A Crazy
Pastor's Wife

~

Halie,
So glad God Sent
you to The Grace Place!
Hope you enjoy the Book!
Love,
Sara   may 2015

A Crazy Pastor's Wife

Wit and Wisdom from Saints and Scoundrels

Joyce Thrasher

Cartoons by Joseph Brown

Scripture quotations from THE MESSAGE, copyright by Eugene H. Peterson 1993, 1994, 1995, 1996, 2000, 2001, 2002. Used by permission of Tyndale House Publishers, Inc.

Scripture quotations marked (NLT) are taken from the Holy Bible, New Living Translation, copyright 1996, 2004, 2007, 2013 by Tyndale House Foundation. Used by permission of Tyndale House Publishers, Inc., Carol Stream, Illinois 60188. All rights reserved.

Scripture quotations marked (NIV) are taken from the Holy Bible, New International Version, NIV. Copyright 1973, 1978, 1984, 2011 by Biblica, Inc. Used by permission of Zondervan. All rights reserved worldwide. www.zondervan.com The "NIV" and "New International Version" are trademarks registered in the United States Patent and Trademark Office by Biblica, Inc.

Library of Congress Cataloging-in-Publication Data

A Crazy Pastor's Wife: Wit and Wisdom from Saints and Scoundrels by Joyce Thrasher
Cartoons by Joe Brown, Editor Jeannie Rogers

Copyright © 2015 Joyce Thrasher
ISBN-13: 9780986102509
ISBN-10: 0986102504
Library of Congress Control Number: 2015901485
Joyce Thrasher, New Brockton, AL

1. Christian Living
2. Ministry
3. Pastors' Wives
4. Marriage

The names of saints or scoundrels in some of the stories have been changed, and any resemblance to anyone living or dead is purely coincidental, accidental, or unintentional, and may be the result of a flawed memory or a vivid imagination.

JET Ministries

THANK YOU

I appreciate everyone who supported me through the process of writing this book. On the days when I wanted to quit, Donny, my soul mate, lover, and best friend encouraged me. My boys Chris, Zach and Noah always give me a reason to smile and new material to write about; they make life so much more interesting. I'm so proud of my sons and can't imagine how boring life would be without them!

I thank my "Peeps," my close friends who supported me though this whole process and had to listen to me talk about "The Book" for hours on end. My mom and dad always encouraged me to be "unique" and not just go with the flow, but to be the free spirit God made me to be. Jeannie, my editor who is an awesome woman of faith, stayed busy on the other end of the phone or computer, editing this book 5,347 times . . . and she is still my friend! Of course, I want to tell my brother Joe how much I love him and appreciate him for helping me realize my dream of being a published author.

Most of all, I thank God for opening windows and doors for this adventure of writing a book for HIS glory!

Joyce Thrasher, January 2015

TABLE OF CONTENTS

JUST A MOM

I would rather raise 100 boys over one girl.

Julie Brown (Joyce's Mom)

Ever feel as if what you're doing isn't important? I know I do.

Now don't get me wrong. Our three boys, Chris, Zach, and Noah, are very grateful and have always been very respectful to Donny and me. At times they depend on us for a lot (which I actually like). Yet, at other times Donny and I feel as if we're not teaching the boys to be responsible and take care of things on their own. I tend to want to fix everything and make everything right. Problem is, I can't do that (and shouldn't do that)!

When my boys were small, so many times, too many times, I told them, "Hurry hurry, we gotta go." I wish now that I had appreciated those moments when they asked me to stop and listen to a story or to play a little longer instead of telling them to "speed it up!" Over the years of my boys' childhood when I was up to my eyeballs in changing diapers, doing laundry, cleaning, and cooking, if I wasn't watching the boys every minute, they would shove pennies up their noses or find an unknown pill to swallow (which ended up being a Vitamin C).

Once when I was at my wits' end, I remember an older woman at the grocery store telling me, "Enjoy those little ones. Before you know it, they'll be grown." I smiled at her with my teeth clenched, all while wearing a white shirt stained with spit up and grape juice and feeding my boys Teddy grahams as fast as they could eat them. Of course, the boys were fighting each other. Zach was almost falling out of the cart and Noah was strapped in the cart seat and crying. I walked away thinking, "That lady has no idea what she's talking about." But now I know differently.

Now that Zach and Noah are older, I'm that woman who says to other mothers, "Enjoy those little ones . . ." Even so, after one particular ER visit when Zach and Noah were teenagers, I said to them, "You're killing me slowly, and if you ever find me dead in a basket of laundry, all my hair pulled out with my cell phone in my hand and the last text was from one of you, you will know that you finally succeeded."

There's no mother on earth who, when she has small children, really enjoys every minute of every age and every stage. I don't care what the "Mother of the Perfect Child at Church" says. I'm sure she has some hissy fits behind closed doors because her little "angel" isn't always that good. ALL children frustrate ALL mothers! And when those same children become teenagers, that's when mothers are really ready for them to "grow up and move out of the house."

I know when ALL my boys finally move out, and when they come back to visit and have time to spend with me, I'll listen closer and cherish the moments we have together. I see how fast they grow up and what a short time I have to teach them. If I had it to do over again, I would slow down and not worry about the house being clean, what was the latest neighborhood gossip, what the boys wore to church on Sunday, or which kids were learning their ABCs or multiplication tables before my kids.

When my boys were small and fell and skinned their knees, I had a bandage for that. When they had a bad or sad day at school, I could bake cookies and make it all better. When another child was mean to them, I listened to their cries and wiped their tears and told them how to cuss in a different language so teachers wouldn't know they were saying a bad word. How was I supposed to know that one of the teachers had just moved back from Germany? That wasn't a nice call she made to the "pastor's wife" about the word Zach said that he told her I told him to say. So as a last resort, I also taught my boys how to speak Pig Latin when they encountered kids who were mean. In fact, I'm pretty fluent in Igpay Atinlay myself! Not sure, though, if this language will help in college.

I once did most everything for my boys, and I thought that as they grew older, the easier it would be. Actually, it's a whole lot harder. When the boys were little, I could dress them however I wanted, make them eat whatever I cooked, and dictate wherever they went. Now I don't have that control. In fact, I don't have much control at all. All I can do is pray that when they make decisions, they'll remember everything Donny and I taught them. I can't tell you how many nights I stay up praying for our boys. Letting go is hard, but I'm not letting them "go." I'm letting them "grow" into the men God wants them to be. I know God loves our boys more than we do.

Donny says I'm a "Mama Bear" and he's right! Yet, I can't always protect my cubs from the hard knocks of life. I wish I could, but then they wouldn't learn some of life's most important lessons. Just as God lets each of us experience some hard knocks in life so we can learn, my boys need to learn the same way. First Peter 1:7 (NLT) says, *"These trials are only to test your faith, to show that it is strong and pure. It is being tested as fire tests and purifies gold - and your faith is far more precious to God than mere gold. So if your faith remains strong after being tried by fiery trials, it will bring you much praise and glory and honor on the day when Jesus Christ is revealed to the whole world."*

When Zach left last year for army basic training after enlisting in the National Guard, it was hard saying goodbye to this young man who so recently was my baby boy. On the morning after he left, I picked up his stuff scattered around the house - three pairs of shoes just in the living room, his underwear on the bathroom floor, and his towel hanging over his bedroom door. As I did that, I cried and threw the shoes and other things into Zach's bedroom and closed the door. Then I realized that Zach was going to be okay. Even though I wasn't with him, God was with him - all the time!

Now Noah will soon be off to college and Zach is making a career of college at this point. But life is good and I enjoy our boys and the laughter they bring to our lives! Chris, our oldest son, recently married Meggie, a true Southern Belle. I enjoy having another woman in the family! I've been out numbered 4 to 1 since the world began. Hmmm; wonder if Meggie picks up Chris's underwear from the bathroom floor?

I know our sons will be just fine. Even so, Donny and I want to love them and protect them and have everything unfold perfectly for them, but we know it's best to let them find their own way. As young adults, they have to figure life out for themselves - and move out of the house. My job description now says, "It's time . . . time to let them go." But that's not easy! After all, I'm just a Mom.

DON'T PULL THE ALARM

*You can learn many things from children: how
much patience you have, for instance.*

Franklin P. Jones

In 1997 Enterprise built and opened a new post office. It
was the talk of the town! The old post office was a few miles
away, behind the courthouse, and it had not been updated
since 1650. Well, at least it looked that way!

I had to mail a package a few days after the Grand
Opening. Zach was four and Noah was one. As a young
mother, and like most young mothers, I dragged my kids all
over town while running errands. I kept Noah strapped in
the stroller and Zach would hold my hand. It usually worked,
but sometimes the boys interrupted my errands. Noah would
get fussy, but I always kept a supply of Teddy grahams and
juice boxes for Noah. My sweet Zach was good about staying
right beside me and I usually didn't have to worry about him
running off and getting into trouble.

When I got to the post office that day, the line was literally out the door. That's when I remembered UPS had just gone on strike. Everyone now had to use the post office to mail their packages.

I was in line for at least thirty minutes; it was moving at a snail's pace. We were about half way to a clerk when Noah began fussing. Unfortunately, I had forgotten to bring inside the snacks and drink boxes which were in my car. As I was trying to calm Noah, I heard the fire alarm go off, and it was loud! I looked up from Noah, and that's when I saw my sweet, 4-year-old Zach standing underneath the bright red fire alarm box with his hand on the pull lever. He was guilty as charged!

The postmaster yelled to everyone, "Evacuate! Evacuate the building now! The fire department is on the way!" Even though I told the postmaster that my son had pulled the alarm, he replied, "Ma'am, this is mandatory procedure. Everyone must evacuate. Now!"

Of course, I was not popular in the post office after that. People looked at me as if I was the worst mother ever. I obviously didn't have control over my kids, or that would never have happened. I quickly left and put both kids in the van where Zach had a little meeting with a wooden spoon I carried in my purse. Needless to say, I did not mail my package that day or even any day that week. I was too embarrassed to go back to the post office. I waited two weeks until the UPS strike was over!

I see this same scenario often played out in my life. At times I've pulled the alarm on a situation. I've jumped to conclusions about a person just because someone told me something about that person. I've made fast judgments and quick decisions without asking God and waiting for His answer. I've believed the gossip when I didn't know the whole truth.

The alarm I pull by being hasty causes a fire truck or two to put out the "fire" I lit by not hearing correctly, by being impatient, or by listening to gossip. I've had to learn this lesson the hard way, and I'm still learning it. And yet, every time I pull the alarm, God gently corrects me. Next time I hope to be more careful.

Wait patiently for the Lord. Be brave and courageous. Yes, wait patiently for the Lord. (Psalm 27:14 NLT)

GUM BUM

*The quickest way for a parent to get a child's attention
is to sit down and look comfortable.*

Lane Olinhouse

Before I became a pastor's wife, I was a pastor's girlfriend. I know it's hard for people to think about or picture their pastor ever "dating," but that usually happens before marriage. And I'd like to mention that when Donny and I started dating, it wasn't love at first sight. It took a full five minutes!

The first time Donny invited me to hear him preach, I was wearing a beautiful light green suit and my two young sons, Zach and Noah, were dressed like "perfect" church boys. I was so excited! We sat on the front row and it all began.

The Army chapel where Donny preached had kneelers because the space was shared with a Catholic service, which occurred later in the morning. My boys had never seen kneelers before; they were very curious. Zach and Noah decided to try out the kneelers, but they couldn't/wouldn't be quiet while doing that because the large, old chapel echoed every noise.

So I attempted to stop the noise-making with some parental bribery - chewing gum that came in a big foil package (I think that's allowed anywhere, even in church). My bribery and distraction with the gum worked and the boys stayed still, chewing gum and writing all over the worship bulletin.

I almost made it through my first church service with my soon-to-be pastor husband without a major catastrophe . . . until the altar call.

During that time as a woman came down the aisle to talk to Donny, there was a commotion behind me, and I felt someone touch my . . . ummm . . . gluteus maximus. Donny also noticed the commotion and saw another chaplain directing the attention of an older lady to my rear end. As Donny tried to focus on the altar call and the woman coming down the aisle, he was also trying to figure out why the other chaplain was so interested in my bottom. Then the older lady tapped me on my shoulder and pointed out the package of gum stuck to my pretty green suit.

Yes, stuck to my "bum" was the whole package of gum for all to see. One of my boys had partially put a piece of chewed gum back into the package and had laid it on the seat for me to sit on. Unfortunately, the gum I bribed my boys with became more of an embarrassment than the noise they made that inspired the bribery.

As Donny finished praying with the woman at the altar, he glanced at me to see what the commotion was all about. I sheepishly held up the package of gum to show him.

That's how my "career" as the "pastor's wife" began. Donny and I still laugh about that story. Since then, many more of what Donny labels "Joyce stories" have happened. That's one thing I love about the ministry - there's always some humor if you look for it, and I always try to find "funny" in situations. Life is just too short to be serious all the time. *For the happy heart, life is a continual feast.* (Proverbs 15:15b NLT)

"It's a women's study on 101 ways to
know your husband in the Biblical sense."

INTIMATE ISSUES

Don't compare your love story to any you watch in movies.
Those are written by screenwriters. Your love story is written by God.

Jennifer Dunn

Wife of the Deputy Post Chaplain (Lieutenant Colonel) Senior Pastor, Wings Chapel, Fort Rucker, Alabama. Yep! That was my first job as a pastor's wife. I had no idea what I was getting into. It didn't take me long to find out!

When Donny and I were first married, not only was he a Lieutenant Colonel in the U.S. Army, he was a General in God's Army. He preached, went to hospitals for visits, performed weddings, baptized people, presided at funerals - the whole nine yards!

Donny decided to serve a small church on post called "Wings Chapel," a beautiful World War II chapel filled with furniture made by German POWs. We shared Sunday morning space with a Catholic service at 11:00 and with a traditional Episcopal service at 8:00; we began our contemporary Christian service at 9:00. This particular type of service was new to both Donny and me. For sure, God had, and has, a sense of humor!

Being an officer's wife and a chaplain's wife, I was quickly thrown into a world of strict rules and regulations. I was 17 years younger than Donny and expected to fit into a circle of women, each of whom had one purpose in life - to be holier than the other chaplains' wives (CWs)! Really? That was definitely going to be a challenge! Looking back now, I realize that even with God's sense of humor, He had a reason for what He put me through to help me learn patience and how to handle people. Case in point:

In the "CWs' Den" (without the lions, of course, but with all the drama of a bad episode of "As the World Turns"), those women knew every single Bible verse and its address (book, chapter, and verse). Each time we met, it seemed as if we played a game of "who is more holy, me or thee." It was so superficial and I had no time for such games with two little boys at home and all the military balls Donny and I had to attend, not to mention hundreds of other Army obligations. And, of course, our number one priority was our ministry at Wings Chapel to the young soldiers and their families.

But I was "fresh meat," not only because I was under 40 years old, but because I didn't wear the official uniform of the CWs (jumpers: long dresses worn over a long shirt, usually in jean material). Plus, I was married to a much older chaplain who happened to be their husbands' boss.

I think the CW gang had "meetings" (or "coffees" as they called them) just to sit around and put pressure on me to answer their prying questions in their "circle of judgment." I was always afraid they would give me a surprise pop quiz about Leviticus or worse yet a Bible verse drill from Revelation!

In addition to the CWs there was a very active group of "regular" military women at Fort Rucker. Five different Bible studies were offered at the same time every Tuesday and at least 100 women attended. We also offered free child care, and a lot Moms attended just to have a two-hour break from their little "angels." Some amazing things happened during those years of Bible study at Fort Rucker. I saw so many miracles and God working in us and through us. Tuesday was the highlight of my week.

Of course, we had opposition from the CW gang and other negative Nellies who were upset about our monthly luncheons and what we were serving and what dishes and tablecloths we were using. I never experienced such a group of women who worried so much about such trivial matters!

Unfortunately, it so happened that all the women in the CW gang were automatically on the official "board" to choose what to study. I wasn't "holy" enough in their eyes to be on the board, but I still gave my opinion (as I always did and always have and always will).

I felt led to teach a Bible study for women about "intimate issues," a study to help women enhance their relationships with their husbands. I asked the board if I could teach that. I stood there in front of all the judgmental eyes looking at me and I stated my case about how young and older women need that study on how to make marriage better, with communication, quality time spent with their husbands without the kids, and, of course, sex.

Oh my goodness, you would have thought I was standing there naked telling the women about that book and actually using that forbidden CW word, sex! I wasn't sure if some of those women had ever had sex although I did know that two of them had sex because they were pregnant ALL the time.

As fate would have it, Donny happened to be the advisor over the women's weekly Bible studies at the chapel. When the CW gang had their board meeting, Donny was there. He wasn't invited, he just showed up. He went to the meeting when they voted on the next Bible studies that would be offered.

One of the CW gang members, who was habitually pregnant and didn't care if her hair was washed or if her clothes were wrinkled, was hiding the forbidden "intimate issues" book under another book. Donny already knew about the CW gang and how they operated. He had been around their type a lot longer than I had.

Donny saw what that particular CW was doing and asked, "What about that book?" All the "holy" women were embarrassed, but the one hiding the book blushed fifty shades of red! She and the other CWs were busted!!

Needless to say, I taught the intimate issues study and we had more women attend that Bible study than any other study that year. And you know what? Women learned a lot in that study about how to be a good wife, to be submissive, to take care of themselves, and to be a helpmate and mother without losing their identity as a woman. They learned it was okay to dress up and go on dates with their husbands without the kids, and yes, to even have fun in the bedroom!

I must admit, I don't miss those days as a CW. I'm so glad God taught me how to relate to other women simply by being myself.

A Crazy Pastor's Wife

Don't copy the behavior and customs of this world, but let God transform you into a new person by changing the way you think. Then you will know what God wants you to do . . . and since we are all one body in Christ, we belong to each other, and each of us needs all the others. (Romans 12:2 & 5 NLT)

"Ten suggestions would be easier to accept..."

THOU SHALT NOT LIE

Children seldom misquote you; in fact, they usually repeat word for word what you shouldn't have said.

Jim Brown (Joyce's Dad)

The summer when Zach was 7 and Noah was 4, I decided to take them on a road trip, by myself and about twelve hours one way. We were fine while driving to our destination and the visit was nice.

On the way home we ran into a little problem. I was driving a bit too fast and wasn't paying attention to what was around me. All of a sudden from the back seat Zach yelled, "Mom, there's a police car with lights on right behind you."

Now something drastic had to be done because I couldn't afford another ticket on my record. I had to think fast as I slowed down to pull off to the side of the highway. I told Noah, "Honey, when the policeman comes up to my window, start crying. Even if you can't, just pretend. Cry really loud." Then I told Zach, "Sweetheart, as soon as the policeman comes to my window, jump out the back door and run into the grass and pretend you're throwing up."

The officer came to my window and informed me I was going 19 miles over the speed limit. As he was talking, Noah started screaming and "crying" and Zach jumped out and began "gagging" in the grass. Frantically I said, "Sorry, officer, I was speeding because I have to find an exit. As you can see, my little boy is very sick."

The officer looked at me like this wasn't his first rodeo and said, "Ma'am, you just sped by two exits."

Yes, I was busted! But the policeman was nice and just gave me a warning. So now I could keep my driver's license a little longer without any more points!

There's no moral to this story. I admit I was wrong and shouldn't have involved my children in deceit. I know that to be true because just a few weeks ago it all came back to bite me. I was riding with Noah (who is now 18) and he was speeding. When we saw a policeman waiting in a cruiser on the side of the road with a radar gun, Noah said to me, "Mom, if this policeman pulls me over, pretend you're sick."

COMMUNION WHINE

*You spend the first two years of your children's lives
teaching them to walk and talk. Then you spend the next sixteen years
telling them to sit down and be quiet!*

Phyllis Diller

When Donny and I first began serving in ministry together, he was still an active duty Army chaplain. At that time we were stationed at Fort Rucker, Alabama, and assigned to the Wings Chapel, one of two churches on post. Donny chose the chapel because it was contemporary and we felt God was leading us into a new kind of worship. In fact, Wings Chapel was the only contemporary church at the time in Enterprise.

Each Sunday we had two services. We were always crowded, with extra chairs set up everywhere. Not only was every chair filled, but so were the "window" seats, which were actually the window sills. We had a lot of young families and their children and a lot of single soldiers. Donny and I had so much fun serving the military.

When we offered communion at Wings, we always tried to have a solemn and quiet atmosphere, giving people time to pray and reflect about the meaning of communion. The trays contained both grape juice and wine so people from different traditions could have their choice.

Because the chapel was so crowded, Donny and I always sat in folding chairs in the very front. Our boys, Zach and Noah, sat in a pew three rows from us. But the way Donny and I sat gave us a clear view of the boys at all times. I could give them "the Mom eye" if they were not paying attention.

One communion Sunday when the wine/juice tray was passed to Zach, who was 9 years old at the time, he decided to ask me in a very loud voice, "Mom, can I have the wine?" I shook my head "No." Not to be deterred, Zach asked again, this time a little louder, "BUT I WANT THE WINE. WHY CAN'T I HAVE IT?"

By then I was very aggravated at Zach's disrespectful and disruptive behavior, not to mention that everyone was looking at us and silently laughing. But Zach, bless his stubborn little heart, kept whining about wanting the wine. At that point I decided it was going to be a case of proving to Zach and to everyone else that I had control over my son. So I looked at Zach with "the Mom eye" and the pressed-together Mom lips and said, "NO! JUICE! TAKE THE JUICE! NOW!"

People started laughing out loud at our little family communion commotion! Needless to say, the solemn and quiet atmosphere of the "communion mood" for that Sunday was over.

Oh, the joys of being in ministry while raising young children! At least they always had a way, and still do, of helping to keep us humble.

A Crazy Pastor's Wife

Train a child in the way he should go and when he is old he will not turn from it. (Proverbs 22:6 NIV)

PRESS 1 TO LEAVE A MESSAGE

Be careful what you say. You never know who is listening.

Joyce Thrasher

As a new Chaplain's Wife (CW), I didn't fit in at all. Only one CW was nice to me; her name was Harriet. She was like a Grandma. She talked to me like I was a real person and didn't just snub her nose and ask me questions so she could talk about me later to the other CWs. I think Harriet was over that and too old to care any more what people thought.

Whenever I walked up on the other CWs talking in a hallway, they would go silent and just look at me as if I were a Zombie. It wasn't always fun being a CW, but I sure did love my "chaplain" as he was the hottest chaplain on Post, actually, in the whole U.S. Army!

One day Harriet and I had lunch together before we went to visit another CW who recently had a baby. It seemed like this particular CW could produce two babies a year. To be honest, I wasn't excited to see what she had this time, another boy to add to their collection of nine kids? Of course, all her kids were "perfect" even as they ran up and down the hospital halls screaming and annoying everyone, including me! It just reminded me why I didn't want any more kids. Not that I don't love kids, but three boys are enough!

As Harriet and I ate lunch, she told me a story about when she was a young chaplain's wife. "There was this one chaplain's wife who wasn't very nice to me," Harriet said. "I had no choice but to work with her on planning events, church functions, military wife obligations, and on and on. One day she really upset me and hurt my feelings. That night I invited a friend over to my house while our husbands worked late. I needed to call this not-very-nice woman to talk with her about an upcoming event. I dreaded having to make the call, but knew I had to do it. So I called her and left a message, asking her to call me back later."

After leaving the message, Harriet told me that she and her friend started talking about that particular CW who was not-very-nice. They both mentioned how much they disliked her and how mean and spiteful she was and yada…yada… yada. A few minutes into their talk, they realized the phone had not been hung up. So everything they said about that woman was now on that woman's answering machine for her to listen to when she got home and for her to share with other CWs and with her husband (who happened to be the boss of Harriet's husband) and with anyone else who would listen!

"What could I do?" Harriet said. "Did her voicemail actually record me? If so, would she hear all those terrible things I said about her? I couldn't break into her house and steal the tape with the message, even though I thought for a minute or two about doing that. I fretted all night knowing I would have to tell my husband how I offended his boss's wife."

Then I asked Harriet, "What happened the next time you saw her? Did she say anything? Do you think she heard it all?"

"Oh yes," Harriet replied, "she heard everything my friend and I said about her. She avoided me from the day she received that message until the day we moved to a new duty station."

Then Harriet, this sweet, older chaplain's wife, looked deep into my eyes, and I leaned forward so I wouldn't miss any words. And she whispered to me, "Joyce, you know what I learned from that situation?"

I thought, "Here it is. The secret! The way to be a real chaplain's wife with some true wisdom from a lady who has been a chaplain's wife for over 25 years."

Harriet said, "Make sure the phone is hung up before you start talking ugly."

I just sat there and waited for her to laugh or say, "I'm just kidding." But no, she was serious! So from that day on I always make sure the phone is hung up before I ever say anything to anyone about anything!

If you keep your mouth shut, you will stay out of trouble. (Proverbs 21:23 NLT)

PERFECT PASTOR'S WIFE ... NOT

People are drawn to you when you're real, not fake.
So be yourself. Everybody else is taken.

Jeannie Rogers

I gave up the title of "Chaplain's Wife" when Donny retired from the military, and I took the title of "Pastor's Wife" at a small, Southern Baptist Church. I was so nervous with this new title (and new job) because you know how church members often find fault with the pastor's wife. I know that first hand because I was once one of those church members before I married a pastor! I now knew there was a target on my backside.

One of the first things I thought I needed to do was buy some "Pastor's Wife" clothes. I went to a store in our town (I won't say the name of the store) which has probably been open since Enterprise was founded in 1896, a store known for its very conservative, older, more mature ladies clothing. When I walked in, I was the only woman without a full head of gray hair. Now don't get offended by this. I know the Bible says that gray hair means wisdom (well, most of the time), but I've met some mean, feisty gray-haired old women and I am sure you have, too!

The ladies working in the store knew just what the "Pastor's Wife" at Salem Baptist Church should be wearing. They fitted me in two suits with skirts just the right length. They also had me buy elastic waist polyester pants and very conservative shirts that showed no cleavage (not even my neck)! I looked like Grandma minus the gray hair, not like the 34-year-old woman I was.

But you know what? Every time I wore the "Perfect Pastor's Wife" clothes, I didn't feel like "ME." And the same thing happened when I tried to act like the "Perfect Pastor's Wife," as if anyone knows how a "Perfect Pastor's Wife" should act! From the ones I've met, I really wouldn't want to act like them anyway. They are pretty boring and don't have my sense of humor.

I also tried to talk like the "Perfect Pastor's Wife." I thought I could throw a few $5.00 churchy words in here and there and I would sound good. As soon as I opened my mouth to laugh, though, that flew out the window (if you have ever met me, you know I have a very distinctive laugh).

I didn't even know how to say "Bless Your Heart" right. I'm originally from the North, and I thought "Bless Your Heart" was a compliment! After I learned that in the South it wasn't, I knew why all the women in the church kept blessing my heart all the time!

So I went on a little mission, interviewing other Pastors' Wives (PWs). They told me the only jewelry I should wear was a cross around my neck. On days when I felt a little rebellious, maybe some cross earrings, but not the dangly kind. The only book I should read was "The Bible in 26 Translations" and I should always be seen carrying it! The PWs told me, "When you go to the grocery store, be on guard. Church members are everywhere and they'll jump out at you when you least expect it, and they'll inspect your cart. So if you want to buy wine, drive over to the next county! Don't buy wine at the local Publix."

When I asked the Methodist PW about this, she said, "Be on guard! If you go to the next county, you'll run into the Baptist pastor's wife who told you that and you'll also run into some of your church members, because we know some of those Baptists drink."

I also had another PW tell me, "Don't show affection to your husband in public, or church members will think you're 'doing it' at home." Well yeah, we are! She then said, "Unless you plan to have a baby, you don't need to do that." I thought, "Well, Donny's too old for that anyway since he's 17 years older than I am (I mean the part about having a baby; he isn't too old for sex)." But I didn't dare tell her that! After getting all the advice from other PWs, I now felt like a criminal - no beer, no wine, no sex, and I guess dancing was out of the question, too!

Then I came up with a brilliant idea! I said to myself, "Joyce, you know what? You can be organized!" All PWs are organized, right? So I read every book and bought every magazine in the check-out lane on *"How to Be Organized in Ten Easy Steps."* Well, the authors of these books and magazines had never seen my house! I even taught a Bible study on how to be organized (which I had no business teaching). I never learned anything from the books and magazines and

I think everyone who bought them just found out how unorganized I really was.

One day as I was trying to color code Donny's sock drawer and alphabetize all the cans in the pantry and turn them just the right way, I realized, "God didn't give me the gift of organization, but He did give me organized people in my life to help me fill the unorganized defect I was born with. Thank You, Jesus!"

I still lose my keys, purse, and phone multiple times a day. I love the iphone finder app. The only problem is I have to first find my computer in order to use the finder app. At times that can be challenging, especially since we don't live in a big house. It's 1,900 square feet, but I'm so talented, I can lose anything in it!

I once lost my phone and keys and Donny found them in the refrigerator. Just recently Donny found my keys, which had been missing for three days, in the freezer in the garage. Every morning before my sweet husband leaves for work, he lines up on the kitchen counter my purse, phone, and keys. He knows if he doesn't, he'll likely get a frantic phone call from me, asking him where they are. More than once he's had to come home in the middle of his busy day to find them. My Donny is a very patient man!

I have a wonderful friend, Carolyn, who always tells me like it is. She is very wise, too, but she hides it under her blond hair dye. She told me, "Joyce, don't buy clothes and try to be someone you're not. Be unique! Be YOU!" She was right! Since then I have embraced her words. I am who God made me with my quirky ways (or as Donny says, my eccentric ways) and my crazy laugh.

I'm not perfect and I can't stress myself about it. I don't want to be someone else or someone people think I should be. I am not the "Perfect Pastor's Wife." And guess what? Other PWs aren't perfect either!

So many people want everyone to think their lives are perfect. They never fight with their husbands, their kids are wonderful, their house is always clean, even their animals are well behaved. Well, let me tell you the truth, their houses may look clean, but they still argue with their husbands. Their pets still shed and have accidents on their clean floors and their kids have issues just like my kids do.

I did not embrace the person God made me to be until I was 34 years old. I am different than everyone else in the whole world. I have gifts the Holy Spirit has given me: to work in my church, to be the wife my husband needs, to be the mom my boys need.

I am not fake, but a real woman with real issues, and just because my husband is a pastor doesn't mean I have to be perfect. I'm also thankful we have changed the name of Salem Baptist Church to The Grace Place Church, a much more appropriate name for a church of imperfect people like you and me!

I want to challenge every woman who reads this to not wait as long as I did to be the "real" you, not someone you think you should be. It doesn't matter if you're young or old, Baptist, Episcopalian, Methodist, or like me "A Believer in Christ." You can start right now being "Uniquely YOU," the person God made you to be - A Daughter of the King!

SERVING WITH YOUR HUSBAND AND SURVIVING

Don't marry the person you think you can live with. Marry only the individual you think you can't live without.

James Dobson

Donny and I have been serving together in ministry for over twelve years, and we have learned a lot about each other and the ministry. Donny actually has been in ministry for 34 years, but I've only been doing this for one/third of that time.

Yet, there are still occasions when I think I know what is best for our church. I always have an opinion. I can always "suggest" a topic for Donny to preach on because I know what he's doing at home that makes me mad! So if he researches the topic and delivers a sermon on it, he will find out that I'm right!

I also know exactly what the temperature should be on Sunday mornings in the sanctuary because I'm usually hot (menopause or peri-menopause, who cares what it is because

I'm always hot). Donny calls these episodes hot flashes, but I just think we need the air turned down. Then Donny points around the sanctuary and tells me to look at all the women who are wearing sweaters and gloves and shivering.

Okay, truth be known, I'm not always right. Yes, I said it, but don't tell my husband I said it! To be honest, Donny is usually right about decisions in the church; he is a very wise and patient man. I like to make rash decisions and he doesn't. Donny likes to ponder and think about an answer for a long time. I'm very antsy; waiting is hard for me to do. I like to get things done. Being from the North, this is ingrained in me, but after living in the South I've learned that it takes longer to get things done in the ministry. Even so, when Donny prays and waits for an answer, it works better that way. But he's older than I am, so I know he's had to slow down a bit!

There are other things I've learned in the ministry. For instance, I can't "work" with Donny. Because of our intimate relationship as husband and wife, I take things too personally. Yes, we can work together on a project, but that's a "give and take" situation and can still be hard to do. Take, for example, our weekly YouTube announcements for The Grace Place.

Donny and I video tape every Monday afternoon at 1:30. Donny just walks over to the sanctuary from his office and doesn't have to put on makeup or fix his hair or change his clothes or make sure he doesn't have a muffin top showing. No, Donny just shows up on time, ready for the camera.

I, on the other hand, have to primp, put on the right makeup, fix my hair, accessorize my earrings, and wear the right clothes so my muffin top disappears (or any other lump that could be revealed when the camera rolls). I'm almost always late to our weekly taping, and by the time I get there, Donny is upset because he has "important" things to do and this YouTube video thing was all my idea anyway, and he says, "Nobody even watches it." Now, when we sit down to start taping, we're both upset. But then we loosen up, and by the end of the announcements we're kissing.

Another hard lesson I've learned: I can't control things. I'm originally from Michigan, not a "Southern Belle." I say words that are often hurtful, but I never mean them in a negative way. I'm just straight forward. I may have lived in Alabama now for over 21 years, but I'm still a strong willed Yankee at heart. Plus, I come from a long line of strong willed women. So this has been a hard lesson to learn - that I have to let Donny make the decisions. But I always give my opinion, believe me, and I don't just sit around and say, "Yes, Honey." When a decision has been made, I stand behind Donny and support him . . . even if I think my idea is better.

Donny and I are great partners in ministry and we enjoy serving together at The Grace Place. We're totally opposite in personality, which makes it even better or more interesting at times. I like to find humor in everything and sometimes Donny doesn't find humor in anything! I think that comes from being a man and being in the military too long.

I've also found my "place," which is women's ministry. I'm so busy with that ministry, I don't have time to worry about the petty things I once worried about in church. God has given me the gift to reach out to women and Donny has received the gift to preach and pastor the congregation in a way I never could. The differences in our approaches are good and we can reach more people for Christ because of these differences.

I encourage all married women to be patient and remember this: your husband is the one who ultimately answers to God. Your husband has a big responsibility to take care of his family, and if your husband is a pastor, he must take care of the church as well. So if you're married to a pastor, be gentle with him and don't talk about church when he gets home from work. Find another way to communicate about church business (maybe by e-mail or text message), but don't do that at home! Keep your home your private sanctuary!

And I (the Lord) will give you leaders after my own heart, who will guide you with knowledge and understanding. (Jeremiah 3:15 NLT)

WAR OF THE ROSES

Going to church doesn't make you a Christian any more than standing in a garage makes you a car.

Billy Sunday

When Donny and I first came to Salem Baptist Church, we held two worship services, one contemporary and one traditional. Some of the older women of the church who attended the traditional service had to have flowers on the communion table or their time at church was ruined. On our first Sunday at Salem Baptist, an older lady walked in and asked Donny, "Where are the flowers?"

Donny answered, "I don't know. I'm not in charge of flowers."

The older lady said "Humph" in a big sigh and went to the back room where the fake flower arrangements had been stored since the 1970s. She brought out a tired, worn out, faded flower arrangement and put it on the communion table. Then, according to her, it was okay for Donny to begin the service (not that Donny was worried about what she thought).

We began with a hymn from the hymnal (yes, we had those back then). Well, another older lady wasn't happy with the flower arrangement, so while we were singing the hymn, she went to the flower storage room and selected a flower arrangement she liked. She returned in the middle of the hymn and removed the first arrangement and replaced it with her choice of flowers. Of course, that upset the first older lady, so during the singing of the next hymn, she removed the second arrangement and put her favorite flowers back on the communion table. It was "Saturday Night Live" on a Sunday morning!

I tried really hard not to laugh, but wasn't entirely successful because it was so funny. And I wasn't the only one laughing. My mom can usually hold her composure, but she was laughing so loud I could hear her. Then others started laughing and the only people still singing were Donny and the song director.

Even though it was funny, it was also sad to see people unable to focus on praising God because of fake flowers. It challenged me to examine my own motives for going to church. If we're not careful, any of us can be guilty of losing focus on God. We can all get in a rut with "church" - the music wasn't good today or someone was sitting in "our chair or pew."

In fact, at The Grace Place we recently rearranged the chairs in our sanctuary. We've been in our new building now for over five years and have never moved the chairs around. You would have thought the world was going to end for some people when they couldn't find "their" seat or "their" row. We had a lot of complaints, but we also had a lot of compliments.

The church has to change, we can't stay the same. God always wants us to change our hearts and our attitudes, and sometimes "mixing" things up can make us realize we have been too comfortable for too long and too focused on the wrong things.

To grow in Christ we have to be uncomfortable. It's not easy examining our hearts and our motives for going to church. But church isn't only a building; church is really outside the building. Are we showing God's love to people or are we impatient and unkind? Do we help those in need or just ignore them, even when the Holy Spirit tells us to do something? It could be to make a phone call to someone who is struggling with depression, marriage issues, and/or children who are not living right. What about the woman at church who recently lost her husband after 50 years of marriage? Send a card or visit her.

The church is not just on Sunday morning for an hour. Church is 24/7, just like Jesus is. He's always available to help us. As believers, let's make a difference in our town and our country and do the right thing. Let's live out church in our everyday life, worshipping God for all His blessings and lessons.

We can make anything petty and distract us from the real meaning of why we attend church - to worship God and be filled up with His love for the week ahead! It's not about us and it's certainly not about the flowers!

The Lord says, "These people come near to me with their mouths and honor me with their lips, but their hearts are far from me. Their worship of me is made up only of rules taught by men." (Isaiah 29:13 NIV)

SMALL TOWN LIVING

The nice thing about living in a small town is that if you don't know what you're doing, someone else does.

Immanuel Kant

I grew up in Kalamazoo, Michigan, a metropolitan area with a population of over 326,000. I moved away at age 18, lived in Germany and then in Tennessee, and for the past 21 years I've lived in Enterprise, Alabama, population 28,000. Enterprise has been a great place to raise my boys, but living in a small town where everybody knows you is a lot different than living where I grew up. In the North nobody wants to "know" you; everybody is too busy. People won't "trust" you in the North as easily as people do in the South.

My family lived in the same house while I was growing up. Back then people didn't move like they do now, across town or to a "better" house. We had the same neighbors for my whole childhood and into adulthood. My parents finally moved to Enterprise to be closer to me and, of course, to get away from the treacherous winters in Michigan. Some of our neighbors were our best friends, others we seldom spoke to due to some differences of opinion that either my mom or dad had with them. As a family, we stuck together and knew who our friends (and foes) were.

In the South, though, it seems that the life purpose of some people is to know all they can about everyone within a twenty-mile radius, and then tell everything they know about everyone to anyone who will listen.

There are also pros and cons about living in a large city versus living in a small town. In a large city you can be more invisible, but that can also allow you to be more inconsiderate. You don't care what people think because you don't know them and are not accountable for your actions. In a small town you have to "be nice," otherwise everyone will hear about the pastor's wife who threw a "hissy fit" at Wal-Mart because the store wouldn't price match or take her coupons. You also have to "speak." I never heard about "speaking" up North, but after living in the South for so long, I understand we are supposed to "speak" to everyone, even if we don't like them. It was a whole new concept to me when I moved to Enterprise. But now I often catch myself saying, "She didn't even speak to me." Really, Joyce?

I can't begin to relate all my personal examples of people talking about Donny and me and our kids and The Grace Place Church. It's both sad and funny at the same time. For instance, if my friends and I go out for a much needed girls' night out, the next thing we know, people in town are spreading rumors about us because we were having too much fun. It's amazing how people think "church" women should not have fun. By the time the gossip train rolls around Enterprise a few times, our night out is so distorted and untrue that we can't even recognize it as being the same event.

The devil is the conductor of the gossip train and people who gossip are just riding the rails, clueless that the devil is using their tongues. Unfortunately, some people will always gossip and there's nothing we can do about that. That is between God and them. At least I can give them something to gossip about! Obviously their lives aren't exciting enough!

Truth is, some people are going to gossip no matter what we do. We just need to make sure we are accountable to God for our words and actions. God knows where our hearts are. The older I get, the less I care about what people say and the more I care about what God thinks. I would rather die with people saying I was a little too loud and had too much fun than to be remembered as the boring pastor's wife who never did anything except dress right and talk right when she went to church, but never made a difference in the community or in anyone's life.

When I do pass away, I would like my tombstone to say, "She Made a Difference." How about you? What do you want your tombstone to say?

THE FALL

Donny, I still fall for you every day.

Joyce Thrasher

Sometimes in life we do things without thinking them through. I tend to do that a lot, and then I think, "Why did I do that?" For instance, the "refrigerator story." For those of you who don't know what I'm referring to, here's Donny's version (my version is a little different, because my version is the truth).

Donny's version, short and sweet: Several years ago Joyce was painting in the kitchen, and she stood on top of the refrigerator to paint, and she fell off the top of the refrigerator.

My version: I wanted to paint the wall above the cupboards and didn't want to move the refrigerator. So I stood on top of it. When I was through painting, I put my leg down and it missed the counter and I fell to the tile floor. I fell on my . . . bottom, rump, bum, buttocks, my you-know-what. But I was okay and kept on painting. Granted, I shouldn't have been on top of the refrigerator and I should have "looked before I leaped," but God kept me safe even when I fell. Also, my not-so-skinny bum helped with the fall! A little bit of a bum saves a lot of pain!

So why was I standing on top of the refrigerator? Because I didn't have a ladder. Donny took our ladder to the church and left it there. Now I'm not putting any blame on anyone . . . just sayin'.

Later that day Donny and I drove to the hospital to visit Ted, a friend and member of our church. On the way I told Donny about my fall from the top of the refrigerator. He said, "When we get to Ted's hospital room, I'll take a look." So we went to visit Ted and a lot of other church members were there as well. We visited in the hospital room for about ten minutes, but I was still in a lot of pain, so I asked Donny, "Can you go to the bathroom with me and look at my butt?" Of course, everyone started laughing, but I was serious! Donny took me to the bathroom and I showed him my bum and the bruises and they were bad! We came out of the bathroom rather quickly and, of course, the guys in Ted's hospital room were laughing about that, saying, "That sure was a quickie." Needless to say, Donny was really embarrassed!

Donny then took me directly to the ER. After explaining two times what had happened, the doctors and nurses laughed and said, "We've never had a patient before who fell off a refrigerator." It really wasn't funny, but they thought it was. After the medical staff regained their composure about my almost "fatal" accident, they finally took an X-ray. They were shocked to see that I hadn't broken my tail bone because I was so badly bruised.

For the next three years I heard sermon illustrations (Donny told that story at least three times a year), jokes about falling, jokes about painting, jokes about youknowwhat, and on and on. I was still having pain in my back and had some tests done and learned I have permanent damage due to the fall.

If only I had had the ladder Donny took to the church. Now I'm not putting any blame on anyone . . . just sayin'.

Who can find a virtuous and capable wife? She is worth more than precious rubies . . . She is energetic and strong, a hard worker . . . She carefully watches all that goes on in her household and does not have to bear the consequences of laziness. (Proverbs 31:10, 17, 27 NLT)

"I occasionally stop by to see what the latest trends are and to check out the competition."

NO FUNERAL FOR
PASTOR'S WIFE

*At the funeral of a church member, as I was standing by
the casket, a woman walked up and said, "Oh look! He's wearing
Auburn colors! War Eagle to the end!"*

Joyce Thrasher

In Ezekiel Chapter 24 God told Ezekiel that his beloved wife, the desire of his heart, was about to die suddenly. The Lord commanded Ezekiel to not mourn over her death as a lesson to Israel to show the Jews that they were not to mourn over Jerusalem when it was destroyed. Any personal sorrow felt would soon be overshadowed by the national anguish of the city's total destruction. The only grief more unbearable than losing a spouse and not being allowed to grieve would be to lose eternal life.

Ezekiel's wife died shortly thereafter and Ezekiel obeyed God's instructions. When the Jews saw Ezekiel's behavior and his silence, they asked him why. He told them they were not to mourn publicly over the destruction of their city and its temple, just as he did not mourn over his wife's death. I'm sure the Jewish women were shocked when Ezekiel could not even accept their casseroles, desserts, and sympathy cards (in the South that may be a sin)!

In Ezekiel's life God came first, then his wife. His wife was his comfort, the one he cuddled with at night, the one he complained to when he had a bad day. She was the one who took his breath away when she walked into a room. She made him smile and laugh. She was a powerful tool in his ministry, his strength, his cheerleader, the one who was always there when nobody else was. This sounds a lot like every other pastor's wife! The qualifications and the job description haven't changed in over 2,500 years!

In the Bible we never read about Mrs. Ezekiel until the 24th chapter, and we never learn her name, just "wife," but not any wife, a "pastor's wife." And then God took her life to prove a point to Jerusalem. Ezekiel would no longer feel her touch on his face, hear her telling him that everything would be okay. Ezekiel would never hold her again and tell her he loved her. Knowing she was going to die, Ezekiel couldn't even spend the day with her before God took her home. Ezekiel kept moving forward and knew that one day he would go to Heaven and see his wife again.

Ezekiel's wife made the ultimate sacrifice and died for her husband's ministry. Her life was given up in order to make a point to a group of people who didn't really care about her or her husband. She had made sacrifices before then, too, because Ezekiel was often gone for days on end doing ministry work for God. She stayed home and kept herself busy with the kids and the laundry (no washers and dryers back then). There wasn't a McDonald's in the city to pick up a happy meal, no Publix or Wal-Mart to pick up something from the deli for dinner. Mrs. Ezekiel did a lot on her own while her husband served God, and she served God at home by taking care of the house and children and respecting and loving her husband.

As a pastor's wife, I, too, respect and love my husband dearly. I protect our privacy, and I protect our children like a mama bear! Donny and I are devoted to our church and ministry. When we think nothing is going right with the church - the roof is leaking, people are upset about the chairs being rearranged in the sanctuary, the sound system is messing up, and on and on - we have to remember that when something good is happening, the devil gets mad and tries to sabotage it in any way he can, through anyone he can, whether in the church or outside the church. If the devil can cause any kind of chaos (since he is the King of Chaos), he will. If he can get a foothold in a person's life, he will use that person's mouth to cause dissension in the church or to hurt us personally.

Given that, realize this.

When the "pastor" stands behind the pulpit, realize that the woman sitting on the front row in the congregation and smiling up at her man has been there with him, not only through the good times, but through the hard times as well. She has given up birthdays, vacations, and family gatherings for him to minister to the church and to people going through crises. She has raised his children and taught Sunday school and Bible studies even when she didn't feel like it. She doesn't share what's going on with herself personally or emotionally, even when she's hurting, so her husband can depend on her to be strong for him. She has made many sacrifices knowing that supporting her husband in the ministry is the right thing to do.

So the next time you see a pastor's wife, give her a hug, and let her know that she is appreciated. Then get out of her way, 'cause she's a busy, busy woman, and has things to do!

Then this message came to me from the Lord: "Son of man, with one blow I will take away your dearest treasure. Suddenly she will die. Yet you must not show any sorrow. Do not weep; let there be no tears. You may sigh, but only quietly. Let there be no wailing at her grave. Do not uncover your head or take off your sandals. Do not perform the rituals of mourning or accept any food brought to you by consoling friends." So I proclaimed this to the people the next morning, and in the evening my wife died. (Ezekiel 24:15-18a NLT)

TEXTING ANGELS

All God's angels come to us disguised.

James Russell Lowell

When you hear the word, angel, what do you envision? Beautiful women flying in the air with blond hair, flapping wings, golden halos, and beautiful voices? Or do you envision cupid with an arrow looking to shoot the next "lucky man?" Or do you not believe in angels at all?

What exactly does the word, angel, mean? In Greek an angel is *angelos*; in Hebrew an angel is *malak*. Both words mean "messenger." So angels are messengers of God (like when a secretary takes a message from the boss and relays it to a co-worker). Angels take messages from God and relay them to us!

References about angels are found in almost every book of the Bible. From Genesis and the Garden of Eden to Revelation and our Heavenly Home, angels appeared to men and women to encourage and inspire, to help and save, but most importantly to deliver a message from God.

For instance, in the Old Testament an angel appeared to Abraham when he was about to sacrifice his son (Genesis 22:11), an angel appeared to Moses when he was appointed to deliver the Israelites (Exodus 3:2), and an angel appeared to Daniel when he was thrown into the lions' den (Daniel 6:22). In the New Testament an angel appeared to Mary and Joseph to announce that they would soon have a baby (Matthew 1:20 and Luke 1:26), a host of angels appeared to the shepherds to proclaim the birth of our Savior (Luke 2:10), and an angel appeared to Jesus to comfort and care for Him after He had been tempted for forty days in the wilderness (Matthew 4:11).

That was then, but now, thousands of years later, it appears that angels don't need to appear. All we need to do to receive or send a message is text on our cell phones. In fact, often it's easier to text than to call or visit in person. I know I'm guilty of this, communicating with a few short, encrypted words rather than having a lengthy conversation.

I have three boys and on a regular basis this is how we communicate! And yet, when my phone beeps or rings and I see that it's Chris or Zach or Noah on the other end, I immediately stop whatever I'm doing and listen to or read what he has to say (even if it's one of my boys in the bathroom at home, texting me for toilet paper). My boys usually text or call when they have something important to share, but more often than not they just want to touch base with the home front (although Zach and Noah also text for money). It always warms my heart to hear their voices or read their texts.

The same thing happened when the angels appeared in biblical times. People stopped whatever they were doing and listened intently (don't get me wrong; my boys are not angels, and they don't listen intently). People knew that angels were messengers of God, and that angels had something vitally important to share.

This is still true today. We must always give God our full attention when we pray, and then we must be silent and still and listen to what He says in return. Each and every day He sends us messages, no, not through a visual angel with flapping wings and a golden halo, but through His Holy Word.

When I was going through a rough time and felt like I couldn't take any more, I was actually sitting on a couch in my home, crying by myself with my computer on my lap. That's the exact moment when my friend Shannon sent me a message that showed up big on my computer screen. She was making the silliest face! She had no idea what I was going through at the time since she had just moved to Maryland, a long way from lower Alabama! But God knew, and He knew just who to use to make me laugh!

Yes, God speaks through friends and family and even through strangers who encourage us and inspire us. We can never know for sure, but as scripture says in Hebrews 13:2, sometimes *we encounter angels without knowing it - angels unaware.*

GOOEY GUMMY BEARS

*Candy is nature's way of making up
for Mondays and PMS.*

Amy Manfra

Zach and I love gummy bears, so often I'll buy a three pound bag of them for us. He likes the green and red ones and I like the orange and yellow ones; it all works out well.

Last year when I opened a three pound bag, I ripped the top too much and the bag wouldn't close again. That evening when we went to church, the gummy bears were left on the kitchen counter, totally exposed in the ripped open bag. When we got home from church, I put them in a Ziploc bag.

A little later Zach and his girlfriend were eating gummy bears, and had consumed almost half of the three pound bag. They commented, "Something's wrong. These gummy bears don't taste right." My brother Joe was visiting from Michigan at that time and he also was eating gummy bears by the handful, just shoving them into his mouth. When he came up for air, he, too, said, "Yeah, these gummy bears don't taste right." Even so, Joe continued to feast!

I don't know why, but suddenly I wondered if my cat had "done his business" on the gummy bears. Sure enough, when I checked (and smelled) the remaining gummy bears in the bag, it was evident that's what had happened. Fluffy had peed on them! At that exact moment, when Zach and his girlfriend had a mouth full of gummy bears, I laughed almost uncontrollably and told them why they didn't taste right. They spit them out immediately. And Joe? He spewed gummy bears out of his mouth and they hit the wall across the kitchen. Really? It was only a little cat dribble!

Sometimes things, just like those gooey gummy bears, look good, but they aren't. That's how sin is. It can look really good on the outside, but when we give in to it, we find out it doesn't "taste" right. So the next time you think about doing something that looks good, but you know it isn't right, think about the gummy bears and remember this: not everything tastes as good as it looks!

Do you like honey? Don't eat too much, or it will make you sick! (Proverbs 25:16 NLT)

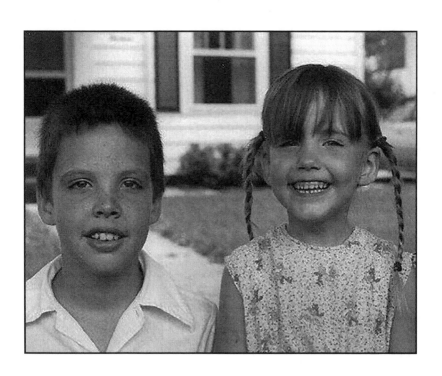

MY "SPECIAL" BROTHER

A brother is the only person in the world who picks on you for his own entertainment and then beats up anybody else who tries.

Joyce Thrasher

So many times we take family members for granted and don't realize how much we need them, and yet, family members seem to always be there for each other in the good, the bad, and the ugly. In my family we don't always agree on everything, but we know that if worse comes to worse, we have each other's back. As the only girl in my family while growing up, I put up with a lot of harassment from my brothers and, of course, being a "daddy's girl," I always got my way! As I've grown up, I've been the family go-between for plans, funerals, and other family matters. I always want to "fix" everything and get everything arranged just right.

My older brother, Joe, who illustrated this book with his cartoons, is very much like me (he denies that). Joe's been through a lot of pain in his life, and during those times I couldn't "fix" everything. But Joe knew I was there for him and always will be. When Joe and I get together, people say we're like twins with our own special language. We may not be politically correct and we both have a unique sense of humor, but we always think we're funny (even if nobody else does)! I'm so blessed to have Joe as my brother and best friend. He's good for Donny, too. Donny can be way too serious at times, and Joe brings out the "laugh" in Donny.

When I was a single mom and went through that hard time, Joe encouraged me and told me it would all be okay. God planned this book and used Joe's talent of cartooning to help me accomplish my dream of being a published author. God is always working and I believe some amazing things are still to come for Joe and me.

Joe and I are what people might call "Radical Christians." We believe God's word is true, absolutely true, without question or doubt. Joe and I also think we can minister "outside the box" because God has His own box and it isn't anything we can create or add to.

I want to thank Mom and Dad for raising us kids in church and for "trying" to keep us on the straight and narrow path. Of course, Joe and I both veered off the path, but we're back! Now we tell as many people as we can about Jesus. Joe shares his faith through humor with his cartoons and with "Pastor Pete," Joe's alter ego. I share my faith with stories on my Crazy Pastor's Wife blog; unfortunately, that's not my alter ego, that's really me . . . crazy!

Two people can accomplish more than twice as much as one; they get a better return for their labor. If one person falls, the other can reach out and help. (Ecclesiastes 4:9-10a NLT)

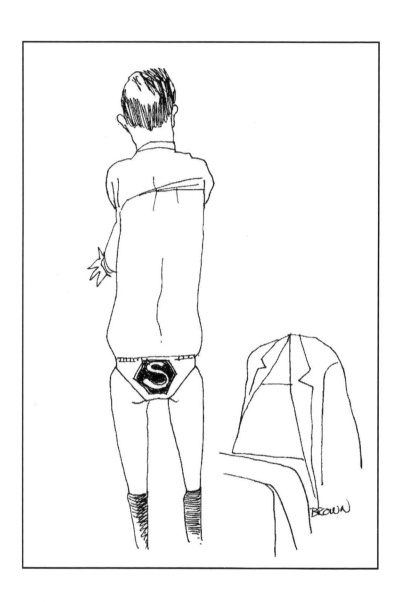

UNDERWEAR AND OVERHEARD

*This morning when I put on my underwear, I could hear
the Fruit of the Loom guys laughing at me.*

Rodney Dangerfield

My husband (like your husband if you're married) often makes me mad. Now since my husband is a pastor, that may shock you! But yes, I do get upset sometimes with my sweet, loving, godly husband. Everyone sees Donny in that perfect light on Sunday morning, but they don't see him at home in his pajamas watching TV with the cat on his head. They also don't see him when he's grumpy. When I happen to get upset, I can be a little passive/aggressive and maybe do things that irritate Donny.

Donny is very organized and must have everything in its "proper place." He can't help it, especially after spending almost thirty years in the military. So several years ago what I enjoyed doing when he made me mad was to put our younger boys' underwear in his dresser drawer. Then, when Donny got up early in the dark, he would get underwear from the drawer so he wouldn't wake me, and sometimes he would get the boys' underwear instead of his. By the time he got the wrong underwear, I had forgotten what Donny had done to make me mad in the first place.

One Sunday morning when it was dark in our room, Donny got underwear out of the drawer, and because he had a baptism at church that day, he got an extra pair of underwear so he would have dry underwear to put on after the baptism.

After the baptism, I went to the "janitor's closet" to check on Donny (as I often did) and found him standing there in our 10-year-old son's underwear. It was quite a sight, especially since Donny still had one more sermon to preach. I knew if he wore that underwear, he would be preaching in a soprano voice, so I quickly left the closet! I never asked Donny what he ended up wearing or not wearing that Sunday when he preached, but he wasn't a soprano.

Needless to say, Donny was very upset with me! I couldn't help but laugh and, of course, that didn't help matters. The good thing was that Donny only had one more worship service to lead that day! I'm glad he wasn't preaching on the scripture from Proverbs 31:28 (The Message) about a virtuous woman, *"Her children respect and bless her; her husband joins in with words of praise."*

Now let me explain why Donny was in the "janitor's closet" changing his clothes. Before The Grace Place moved into our new building, our old building was very small, and we had to use every square inch of space. When Donny baptized people in the old building, the only place for him to change clothes was in a cramped janitor's closet located under some stairs. After a baptism Donny would go to the closet and change for the rest of the service. He was always in a hurry because at that time he was the only pastor at The Grace Place. He had to start the service, perform the baptism, pray for the offering, and, of course, preach.

After a baptism I usually would sneak back to the closet and harass him just for fun. I often said things a wife may say to her husband to flirt, not public flirting but private flirting (if you know what I mean). One Sunday when I did that, Donny and I didn't know his microphone was still on, and as we were flirting with each other, the people in the sanctuary overheard us. Thank God for good sound techs because they were quickly able to mute the mic before Donny and I said anything that would embarrass us any more than we already had (at least I think they did). Even so, we got some funny looks when we came into the sanctuary after our flirting rendezvous.

When I think about that Sunday, it reminds me to always be careful about what I say because I never know who could be listening.

Whatever you have said in the dark will be heard in the light, and what you have whispered behind closed doors will be shouted from the housetops for all to hear! (Luke 12:3 NLT)

Meeting up with Rex, Adam immediately counted his ribs.

HIS RIB

*Do everything you can to preserve and protect love
so that it endures forever.*

Jennifer Smith, unveiledwife.com

As my friend, Stacy, and I were brain-storming about a name
for a conference I'm planning for pastors' wives, she came
up with "His Rib." I immediately latched on to that name
because we, as women, were initially created from "his rib."
In the account of Adam and Eve found partially in Genesis
2:18-24, *the Lord God said, "It is not good for the man to be alone.
I will make a helper (companion) who is just right (suitable) for
him"*. . . *So the Lord God caused Adam to fall into a deep sleep.
While he slept, the Lord God took out one of Adam's ribs and closed
up the opening. Then the Lord God made a woman from the rib
and brought her to the man. "At last!" Adam exclaimed. "She is
part of my own flesh and bone of my bones"* . . . *and the two were
united as one.*

I looked up the meaning of "rib" in the dictionary and
found a definition I really like: "A rib helps protect our

hearts and other internal organs from injuries. For instance, should someone hit us in the chest, the rib cage will save the heart."

Since "his rib" is an integral part of every wife's makeup, that means that we are called to protect our husbands' hearts. Not always easy, though, especially in ministry where our own hearts are broken on almost a weekly basis. Nothing hurts me more than when a person makes a derogatory remark about Donny's preaching or about the way he handled a particular situation in the church. I get so defensive and upset! But those emotions won't help Donny or the church, so I have to watch myself and try to keep my mouth shut.

As a wife, I think it's instinctive to want to defend my husband and tell people why he handled a situation in a certain way. Truth is, people often see a situation only from their little window, not from the big window. So no matter what I say, they won't understand. I know God holds our ministry in His hands, but sometimes the urge is so strong to put people in their place and not take their negativity. Even so, Proverbs 10:19 (NLT) convicts me to do otherwise: *"Don't talk too much, for it fosters sin. Be sensible, and turn off the flow!"*

As "his rib," as the wife of a pastor, I must always strive to protect my husband. As "His rib," as a child of God, I must also strive to protect the church and make sure I'm diligent in setting a good example and loving people in spite of shortcomings (theirs and mine). Knowing that a few wrong words spoken in haste could cause lasting damage, I must continually be true to God's commands so that the heart of His faith-filled church remains steadfast and strong.

At the same time, I must be sure that the heart of my sweet husband remains safe and secure. And even though I like to think I'm the one "guarding" Donny's heart, it is actually God who takes care of that.

THANKS, MOM

Give your mom a call. Tell her how much you love her.
You may be the only person in the world who has heard
her heart beating from the inside.

Suzanne DenBesten

When I was a teenager, I was very rebellious and very disrespectful to my mom. After all, I knew so much more than she did, especially since she was so old and out of touch. All she ever did was go to church, serve in the church, read the Bible, and pray. Oh, and she also cleaned and cooked and did laundry and ran errands and took care of my dad and my two brothers and me.

I usually did what I wanted and often hung out with people who didn't make the list for Mom's approval. Of course, she knew nothing about that. She was clueless - or so I thought! Looking back now, I realize she knew. She knew everything! There's never been a teenager who didn't leave "clues" as to what he or she was doing.

One night when I was 17 years old, I went to a place where I shouldn't go (Mom told me not to go there) and did things I shouldn't do (Mom told me not to do them). I looked at my watch; it was 3:15 a.m. and I was in serious trouble! So I began to pray, and prayed harder than I had ever prayed before, begging God, "Please let me live. If you do, I promise to never go here and do this again. But if I die, please forgive me for my sins and take me to Heaven."

The next morning when I got home, Mom met me at the front door. "Where were you," she asked, "and what were you doing at 3:15 this morning?"

I was shocked to say the least. How did she know? She's not supposed to know anything! I was silent for a minute, and then in a sassy teenage voice I answered, "Nowhere and nothing."

Mom replied, "I was awakened at exactly 3:15 and knew I needed to pray for you. Something was wrong. I got out of bed and knelt down and prayed for over an hour. Then I felt God's peace and went back to sleep."

I held my composure, but wanted to cry. And when I did cry later that day, I finally understood the depth of both God's love and my mother's love. Thinking about it even now makes me tear up.

Over the ensuing years I've come to realize that not only is my mom a wise woman, she's a woman who listens when God speaks. She knows what's right and wrong, what's black and white, and she lives her life accordingly. Because I'm more of a gray, in-between person, Mom and I don't always agree on things, but truth is, I love her dearly, just the way she is!

In fact, I now do everything she did! I clean and cook and do laundry and run errands and take care of my husband and three boys. I also go to church, serve in the church, read the Bible, and pray - a lot!

If it wasn't for my mother, I might not be here today to write this story. I've never told her how she changed the direction of my life in those early morning hours when I was 17. She'll read it for the first time in this book.

So thanks, Mom.

I'm so glad you're you - just a mom.

Listen, my child, to what your father teaches you. Don't neglect your mother's teaching. What you learn from them will crown you with grace and clothe you with honor. (Proverbs 1:8-9 NLT)

"All I saw was an Alabama license plate."

OVER THE RIVER AND THROUGH THE WOODS

Any man can be a father, but it takes someone special to be a Dad.

Anne Geddes

My dad and I often take road trips together. Nobody else ever wants to go with us. We invite them, but they won't come. We don't understand. Maybe it's because Dad and I are a lot alike in that we don't know right from left, how to read a map, or which way is North, South, East, or West. Yes, it has become easier for us to navigate because of the GPS, but this story took place before that technology kicked in.

Several years ago Dad and I wanted to visit Joe who lives in Michigan. So we rented a car to drive to Kalamazoo and back (a 15-hour drive, one way, by the way). The car was very very small, not the big ol' Cadillac my dad usually drove.

We started out on our journey and what a journey it was! The 15-hour drive turned into more like 20 hours (Gilligan's Island tour, part II). We had to fill up on coffee and, of course, that meant we had to stop at more rest areas, and the cycle went on and on. We drove straight through and when we arrived in our "home town," Dad and I actually got lost. Kalamazoo is a big city, not a small town like Enterprise. We called Grandma and by the time we arrived, we were exhausted.

Whenever we visited in Michigan, we always stayed at Grandma's house. She lived in a small two bedroom cottage in a neighborhood of elderly people. Dad slept in the extra bedroom and I slept on the couch in the living room, or as people in the South call it, the den. Grandma was a hoot and full of life. We would laugh and laugh until late at night about old family stories. Grandma cooked so much food when we visited and was always happy to see us. It was the best place to be - "Grandma's House."

On this particular visit, first night there Dad and I went to our respective rooms to sleep. About ten minutes later it started. It sounded like a train, a tornado siren, and a cat in heat all at the same time! What in the world? Grandma had learned how to snore! The noise was so loud, it could be heard outside. It made sleeping very difficult. After visiting for a week, Dad and I were both exhausted, not only from lack of sleep, but from running all over western Michigan to visit Joe and his family and friends.

The night before Dad and I left to head back home, I spent that evening with Janet, a friend I hadn't seen in a long time. We stayed out pretty late reminiscing about old times, and then Janet came into Grandma's house and we laughed and talked until way past 3:00 a.m.

That morning Dad and I planned to leave at 6:00 a.m. So after an hour and half of sleep on my part, we took off for our trip back to Alabama. Dad didn't want to drive, so I drove on nothing but strong coffee and a desire to get home a.s.a.p. By the time we hit Kentucky, I was tired and worn out. We had just finished driving through Indiana, which was a boring ride, nothing but corn fields and flat ground. No offense to the Hoosiers, but the Indiana landscape isn't all that exciting.

As I continued to drive, I wasn't sure if I was seeing a mirage up ahead, but I thought I saw a woodchuck crossing the road. I remembered what Dad had always told me, "Don't ever swerve to miss an animal. If one is in your lane, just go ahead and hit it because you could get into an accident trying to avoid it and slam into another car or worse, flip your car over."

Now, I'm sure Dad meant big animals or deer which are often seen on roads in Michigan. So when I saw that wood-chuck in front of me, I have no idea why I did this . . . and if you're a member of PETA, please stop reading right now! I floored the gas and hit that woodchuck straight on! In that very very small car we had rented, it felt like we hit a deer! The car jumped up into the air and it sounded like the whole bottom of the car was being torn off.

Dad screamed, "WHY DID YOU DO THAT?"

I screamed back, "BECAUSE THAT'S WHAT YOU TOLD ME TO DO – HIT THE ANIMAL AND NOT SWERVE TO CAUSE AN ACCIDENT."

Dad then said, "But I never told you to hit the gas and accelerate to hit an animal!"

Years later, I still feel bad about that poor woodchuck. I'm not really sure why it all happened - lack of sleep for a week while Grandma snored, going back and forth across town to visit my brother, yakking with friends for hours on end, driving numerous hours without a break, or drinking too much caffeine. I have no excuse other than that woodchuck should have been chucking wood like the riddle goes, and not trying to cross the road (that's the chicken riddle)! Since then I've NEVER intentionally tried to hit any animal. Dad still tells this story whenever he has an audience. But he doesn't tell anyone that he refused to drive on that trip back from Michigan!! He has the memory of an elephant!

The Bible says in Ephesians 6:1-3 (The Message), *"Children, do what your parents tell you. This is only right. Honor your father and mother . . . so you will live well and have a long life."*

'nuf said.

Why as a general rule Pastors are not allowed to help on building work days.

WHAT PART OF THE BODY ARE YOU?

*When I stand before God at the end of my life, I would hope
that I would not have a single bit of talent left, and could say,
"I used everything you gave me."*

Erma Bombeck

If you're a wife or a mother or a single woman, do you ever
feel overwhelmed by what God has called you to do? Do you
ever feel inadequate, ill prepared, or unworthy of the task? If
so, remember that God will equip you just as He equipped
Moses who was called to lead a group of stubborn people
through the desert to the Promised Land; or just as He
equipped Mary who, as an unmarried teenage girl, was called
to carry our Savior. No matter the task God has for you, He
promises to equip you if you're willing to submit yourself to
His plan for your life. The scary thing is to submit.

Submitting means that you'll let God lead your life and
that you're willing to do whatever He calls you to do or go

wherever He calls you to go. Now that doesn't mean you're called to sell everything you have and move to Africa as a missionary. Yes, for sure, some of us are called to be missionaries, but others of us are called to minister in our local community. If you fit into that latter category, then focus on that right now.

Maybe God has called you to start a Bible study or a prayer group. Maybe you've been called to serve people by feeding the hungry or cleaning a house or mowing a lawn or maybe by driving someone to the doctor or possibly just by being a listening ear to a person in need. God calls people to do so many different things. That is how the "body of Christ," the Church, works.

The Grace Place has a food pantry and clothes closet that is open two days a week. We have volunteers who are called to stock food, organize clothes, and give their time serving people when the "Manna House" is open. If we didn't have people willing to submit to "their calling," we couldn't stay open. I've heard so many stories of needy people coming into the Manna House, and how our volunteers, who have the chance to serve them, are blessed in return!

One of our members is an "extreme coupon-er." She buys products for the food pantry and also for our senior adults who are on limited, fixed incomes. She has helped so many people with everyday needs by responding to God's call to serve Him in that unique way. We have people with a talent for cooking who use it at church to serve God. In doing so they bless many and are blessed in return for doing what God calls them to do. We have a quilters' group that makes quilts for people in wheelchairs, and we have a lady who crochets blankets for the homebound and for those going through chemo. Some women in the church have the gift to teach or encourage others by sending post cards. We also have prayer warriors, faithful people who are called by God to intercede for others in prayer. So many of these prayer warriors tell me they pray every day for protection for Donny and me and for our church.

I remember one week when Donny and I were feeling down and had been hurt by some "church" people who had made negative remarks about our boys and us. We went to the hospital to visit Mrs. Elaine, one of the older ladies in our church who had undergone knee replacement surgery. When we walked in, she looked at us and immediately asked, "What's wrong?"

We told her we were having a bad week and were feeling pretty low. She said, "Let's pray about that right now."

There was Mrs. Elaine, in pain and in traction, and she prayed for us. We laughed after the prayer and said, "We came here to pray for you."

She replied, "God sent you here so I could pray for you."

I love our prayer warriors!

All believers in Jesus are called, in some way, to serve God. Even if you think your calling is insignificant, answer His call and do it! Anything God calls you to do is important! Being the hands and feet and heart of Jesus is top priority, no matter the task.

He is the one who gave these gifts to the church: the apostles, the prophets, the evangelists, and the pastors and teachers. Their responsibility is to equip God's people to do his work and build up the church, the body of Christ, until we come to such unity in our faith and knowledge of God's Son that we will be mature and full grown in the Lord, measuring up to the full stature of Christ. (Ephesians 4:11-13 NLT)

MIRACLES STILL HAPPEN

*Never measure God's unlimited power by your
limited expectations.*

From "Our Daily Bread"

How many times have you been excited about a miracle that occurred in your life and had someone "burst your bubble" with a pin prick? This has happened to me many times, and it is so wrong. When other people have miracles occur, instead of being negative, we should rejoice in God who is always working. Sometimes we have to look around to see Him.

When Zach was 2 years old, he was diagnosed with a genetic blood disorder. The hematologist said, "This diagnosis is for a lifetime. There is absolutely no cure." Even so, when Zach was 17 years old, he wanted to join the National Guard or another branch of military service. However, since he had the blood disorder, Zach and I knew he wouldn't be able to pass the physical. Yet, something inside me (God's nudge) said, "Take Zach to the doctor and have him re-checked."

So I called the doctor's office to set up an appointment, and a nurse rudely told me over the phone, "There's no way Zach can be cured of this blood disorder. It's just not possible."

I boldly told the nurse, "All things are possible with God. He is bigger than this blood disorder. If God chooses, He can cure Zach." A few days later as Zach and I sat in the doctor's office waiting for the blood tests to be performed, we held hands and prayed for a healing.

Two weeks after the appointment I received a call from Zach's doctor. He asked us to please come back to his office. When we arrived back, the doctor told us, "I don't understand this, but Zach doesn't have the blood disorder any more."

I replied, "It's a miracle! God healed Zach!"

The doctor just sat there, shaking his head in disbelief, "This has never happened before."

I told him, just as I told the nurse, "I serve a big God!" I was excited, giving God the glory, and couldn't wait to tell everyone I met! Zach was apprehensive and wanted to see the test results. He read them and realized that the blood disorder had disappeared.

A few days later when I went to the Bible study I was attending, I shared this miracle with that group of women who seemed to be "deep and spiritual," but who didn't seem to be excited about anything except the Old Testament temple and the laws. Now, don't quote me on that because I have nothing against those things. It's just that I enjoy Bible studies which are more related to today and which encourage and help me serve God better. Yes, I know studying the laws and how the temple was built is important, and I'm sure some people enjoy learning that way, but in this case it was with outdated videos from a lady speaking 25 years ago.

I recently watched a few of those old videos, and I became distracted and thought, "Look at her makeup! Did we really wear that much blue eye shadow back then? Did we really wear our hair in that monstrous beehive style? Yes, she definitely has had plastic surgery done. She looks much older 25 years ago than she does today." Then I began trying to figure out what she has had done.

After telling the Bible study class about Zach's miracle, one of the women said to me in a snide, sarcastic way, "Why do things like this happen to you and your family and never to me or my family?" I was put off with her comment, wondering if she wanted me to answer that question or if she was mad at God who worked a miracle. Maybe she didn't believe it was a miracle; maybe she just didn't like me.

But I felt sorry for her; I looked into her eyes and all I could see was sadness. I told her, "Because we serve a big God, and He's in the miracle business." I thought telling the Bible study women about Zach's miracle might help them make some spiritual movement in their hearts and faces, but all of them still had the pursed lips and the sadness in their eyes.

Unfortunately, there will always be people who question what God is (or isn't) doing. When I encounter such negative Nellies, I think about Jesus. He performed almost forty miracles (which are recorded in the Gospels) and still people grumbled and complained and didn't understand. Jesus could have let those people take away the joy of the miracles and the lives He changed, but He refused to listen. Instead, He rose above the fuss and fray and kept moving forward with

His mission on earth, in spite of the judgment and physical and verbal abuse He took. Because of Jesus' example, all of us should be able to put up with such negative people. We should just give them a BIG smile and keep moving forward with the business of our Heavenly Father!

I want to be a woman who people look at and say, "She has joy! What's different about her and her life? I want what she has." Then I can share with them that Jesus died on the cross and was resurrected so we can go to Heaven and live with Him for eternity!

If we can't "Jump for Joy" knowing that, we may want to check our pulse. Like the ladies in the Bible study, we may be spiritually lifeless.

Oh, what a wonderful God we have! How great are his riches and wisdom and knowledge . . . For everything comes from him; everything exists by his power . . . To him be glory evermore. (Romans 11:33 and 36 NLT)

KEYS UNDER THE CASKET

If God had intended for us to follow recipes,
He wouldn't have given us grandmothers.

Linda Henley

Being in the ministry for the last twelve years, I've noticed that many people in this type of service take themselves way too seriously. I've tried not to do that. And yet, many times I've needed to be serious because I had to deal with a crisis. I've cried with moms who lost children, helped women when their husbands left them homeless with children, took wives to the hospital for surgeries when their husbands were at war, and listened to women tell their stories of hurt, pain and suffering.

Life is not easy, yet sometimes we just need to step back and find something to laugh at. In that light here's a story nobody knows except Donny and me. My family may be surprised . . . well I know they will be if they read this book.

I was devastated when my Grandma Powers died. It was unexpected. We were close and had talked daily. When she died, Donny was asked by my family to speak at her funeral.

After the funeral Donny and I were waiting in a car to go to the cemetery. It seemed to be taking a long time. Since Donny and I have been to many funerals, we felt that something wasn't right. Maybe because we were in the North?

The hearse was directly in front of us and we saw quite a commotion with the funeral directors and the hearse driver. So I asked Donny, "Go and see if you can find out what's going on."

Donny walked over to the funeral director to find out. Then Donny came back and told me, "They've lost the keys to the hearse and think the keys are under Grandma's casket. They're trying everything possible to get the keys out without having to take the casket out of the hearse so it won't upset our family."

I laughed, "Grandma would think this is funny. She always had a good sense of humor."

They finally got the keys out, and in that moment I realized there is usually some humor in every situation. We just have to look for it. Without being disrespectful to Grandma, I believe she would rather have us smiling and laughing than crying and grieving.

I hope when I die, people will find something to laugh about and not be sad because I will be in heaven with Grandma!

A cheerful heart is good medicine, but a crushed spirit dries up the bones. (Proverbs 17:22 NIV)

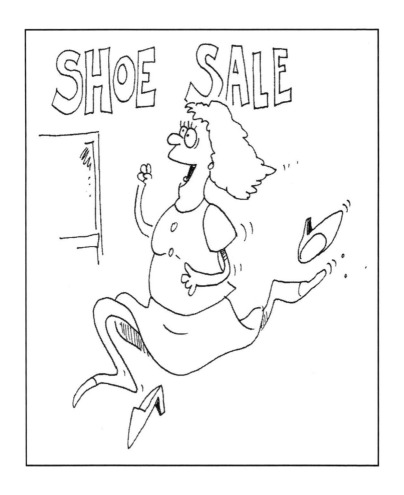

STILETTOS, SANDALS, AND SNEAKERS

Cinderella is proof that a new pair of shoes can change your life.

Dawn Johnson

When you think about your shoes, do you ever think about peace? If you're like me, you probably think, "Can I walk all day in these stilettos and not limp in pain?" or "How long can I wear these sandals without getting blisters?" or "Do these sneakers go with this jacket and jeans?" You probably never think about the definition for shoes, but in our "spiritual armor" the definition is peace.

Ephesians 6:10-15 (NLT) says, in part, *"Be strong with the Lord's mighty power. Put on all of God's armor so that you will be able to stand firm against all strategies and tricks of the Devil . . . For shoes, put on the peace that comes from the Good News so that you will be fully prepared."*

The main battlefield for spiritual warfare is in the mind. The devil loves to keep us confused, worried, and anxious. If he can do that, we have no peace. And if we have no peace, we're no good for service in the church or any place else; we're useless and right where the devil wants us to be!

Just imagine if we tried to run a race in high heels. After the first few steps, we would slow down and then we would eventually fall or quit. But, if we have a good foundation of peace or "stable shoes," then we aren't as tempted to fall and quit. Even so, eventually we will face trouble, so we must never forget Who is in charge. We need to keep doing what God calls us to do. We can't hunker down into our own miserable holes and whine about how unfair life is! No, we must continue serving and loving people. If we stop serving, we're no good for the calling God places on our lives, no matter what that calling is. None of us can ever do that perfectly all the time, but with each experience we should learn something new for the next time we face a similar situation. God is ultimately in control, and even if we think we are, we aren't.

God can choose to let Satan "test" us, and when that happens, we can either attempt to fix things on our own or we can rely on God and the signs He sends our way. Yes, He sends signs to encourage us daily in our troubles, maybe through a person, a word, a verse, a song, a billboard, or even a text from a good friend. If we look, we'll see that God is near and dear, always encouraging us. He wants us to be better and grow and learn to trust Him.

When we're anxious, confused and unfocused, we're not good examples to unbelievers. They think, "Why should I become a believer? Look at them! Their lives aren't any better than ours. They're upset, mad, and worried all the time.

They're not even happy." As Christian women, we need to be examples of peace to others.

Several years ago when Donny was diagnosed with bladder cancer, I remember consoling so many people after they learned about his illness. For some reason Donny and I had peace. We talked about why we weren't anxious or upset and discovered it was the *"peace that passes all understanding"* promised by God in the Bible. I had never experienced peace to that level before, but after Donny's diagnosis, I understood it completely! Donny and I knew God was in control and we were not! We didn't know if God would cure Donny or if we were facing a long battle with cancer, but we just had peace.

It's the same thing right now. God is in charge of life and death and even if we worry about it, the outcome doesn't and won't change. We just give our lives to God, every day, all day!

So the next time you pick out your shoes for an outfit, whether they be stilettos, sandals, or sneakers, think about wearing the shoes of peace, and not the shoes that will hurt after an hour – unless, of course, they're really really cute!

Don't worry about anything; instead, pray about everything. Tell God what you need, and thank him for all he has done. If you do this, you will experience God's peace, which is far more wonderful than the human mind can understand. His peace will guard your hearts and minds as you live in Christ Jesus. (Philippians 4:6-8 NLT)

NO CRUISE CONTROL

You know your children are growing up when they stop asking where they came from and refuse to tell you where they're going.

P. O'Brien

Chris loves fast cars. He always drives the latest models. He lives in Atlanta, dresses nice, and is adventurous. Chris and Meggie scuba dive, travel constantly, and enjoy any new endeavor they can find. Zach and Noah always say, "Chris is the 'coolest' brother ever!"

Whenever Chris gets a new car, he always comes to Enterprise and lets the younger boys drive "The Car." The first car the boys drove was an Infiniti G37. Little did I know that when my responsible son, Chris, took the boys out to drive on the country roads, they drove a little too fast.

Noah got the G37 up to 103 mph and Zach got it up to 100 mph. Zach took a curve too fast and Chris had to talk him through "controlling the situation" so as not to lose control. Thankfully, Chris is an air traffic controller at one of the busiest airports in the country and can think fast in a dangerous, emergency situation. Zach's first reaction, of course, was to hit the brakes, which was not the right thing to do or he would have lost control.

Then Chris bought a Porsche Panamera S and came to Enterprise. Thankfully, Zach was in Texas, training with the Army to be a medic (I think we need a medic in the family, and a psychiatrist would also be nice)! But Noah was still here and very excited to drive a Porsche!

Chris and Noah went for a ride, and Noah got the car up to 107 mph! I only know how fast the boys were going because I recently asked Chris about it. He sang like a canary and confessed to the crimes! Had I known earlier, I would have had a heart attack right where I was standing. Donny would have had a heart attack, too; he has an old ticker anyway! It would have served all three boys right to realize that they were the cause of our early deaths and that they would have to plan a double funeral.

Parents rejoice when their children turn out well . . . So make your father happy! Make your mother proud! (Proverbs 23:24-25 The Message)

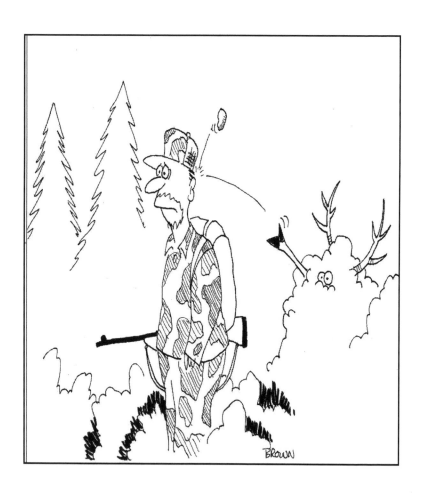

DEER DYNASTY, THRASHER STYLE

If you need 100 rounds of ammo to kill a deer,
maybe hunting isn't your sport.

Elayne Boosler

Once a year the Thrasher house turns into a "Man Hunting Week" of frenzy! Joe flies in from Michigan and Chris drives in from Atlanta. During those seven days of hunting, I have more testosterone in my house than any one woman should ever have to tolerate.

Chris always has the "latest" in hunting equipment. He researches extensively and even buys just the right laundry soap so as not to scare the deer away! Tide won't do, nor will any soap with a nice, fresh fragrance! Chris also has just the right guns, bullets, scopes, clothes, and last but not least, deer pee. Yes, you read that right, deer pee. Apparently it is used so bucks will follow that scent and think there's a doe in heat. I'll spare you the more intimate details of that subject.

If the buck happens to follow the trail of pee to Chris, we'll have deer meat in our freezer for a year. However, if the buck follows the trail of pee to Joe, the buck will live for at least another day. Joe hasn't killed a deer in over five years. He always blames his pitiful shooting on the scope on Donny's gun (which Joe uses). Last year Donny bought a new scope and had it zeroed in perfectly and Joe still missed a deer that had tapped him on the shoulder.

Chris also has motion-sensored cameras which he hangs around the property to be hunted. He video tapes at night when the deer are out. All the men look at the videos and see the deer and talk about how big the antlers are, "Why, he must be a 10 point!" If you ask me, that is called Deer Porn!

Before the big hunt, the men gather around the kitchen table, cleaning their guns and talking excitedly about the next few days. They spread out their gear: gadgets, head lamps, boots, ammo, and camo. Hunting is a huge event in our house, like Christmas Eve, and the men are 5 years old!

They plan what deer stands they're going to sit in and who will get the little shooting house. Whoever gets that is lucky because the house has a propane heater for warmth. The men wake up at 4:00 a.m. and drive to the Big Little to get biscuits and coffee "to go." Then they head out to the happy, hunting ground (about thirty minutes away).

When they arrive there, they have to "mark" with a washer on a wooden board with a diagram of the property. That is very serious and organized hunting because they need to let others in the Hunting Club know where they'll be on the property. Donny is the president of this Hunting Club. I always tell him, "Just think how good this will look on your resume!" I personally call it the "Old Man Hunting Club." If you see any of the members, don't tell them I said that.

Zach has no interest in hunting. He's gone a few times, but he would rather sleep in and not get cold and itchy in the woods. Noah is always excited to go hunting with the men. But bless his heart, Noah always sits next to Donny and manages to fall asleep after he gets warm (Noah is always too cold). One morning Noah was sleeping by Donny in the tree stand when Donny saw it, the big buck from the video camera the night before. Donny placed his finger on the trigger, pulled gently, and shot. He missed the deer, but Noah woke up suddenly to a LOUD gun blast going off in his ear.

Since then Noah always tells Donny to wake him up in the morning to go hunting, but when Donny knocks on Noah's bedroom door to go, Noah says, "I'm too tired, maybe next time." That could be because of the gun blast, the 4:00 a.m. wake up call, or the cold, but Noah hasn't been hunting since that day.

On one of the hunting trips Chris killed a coyote. Now that may sound awful to you, but such is encouraged year 'round in Alabama because of the damage a coyote can do on a farm. Unfortunately, Zach and Noah were asleep when Chris and the others returned from their big adventure. Chris wanted his brothers to see the coyote, so unbeknownst to me, Chris put it in the chest freezer I had in the garage.

The next morning when we all got up, Chris took the boys out to the freezer to show them his kill. Overnight something had happened, and the freezer stopped working. When Chris opened that freezer, the whole garage smelled of two day old dead coyote. You think rotten fish smells bad? Little do you know . . .

Needless to say, I told Donny and Chris and Joe, "Get that freezer out of the garage and find someplace to dump it." They did and since then I fill my new freezer so full during hunting season that there's no room for any kind of animal that might need to be put on ice.

I always love hunting season. I make beef chili and beef stew and feed the hungry, lucky or not so lucky, hunters.

Now then, get your weapons – your quiver and bow – and go out to the open country to hunt some wild game for me. (Genesis 27:3 NIV)

CAUGHT IN THE ACT

*Be careful what you do. It could end up
on YouTube for the whole world to see!*

Joyce Thrasher – said to all three of her boys

Let me start out by saying that my kids definitely are not perfect. They're like all other kids - funny, upbeat, silly, messy, moody, smart, not-so-smart, clever, sassy, etc., but all three are the best looking men in the world! They truly are blessings in our lives and they give Donny and me so much laughter, and sometimes pain!

When sweet Zachary, who is now 21, was a senior in high school, he was an honors' student, summa cum laude, captain of the soccer team, and teachers' aide. He made all the school announcements over the intercom every morning. He never got into any trouble in school; he was the student every teacher wanted to have in class. He did make one big mistake, though. One morning while making announcements, he was supposed to say tomorrow is "Dress for Success Day"

Joyce Thrasher

and instead he said "Dress for SEX Day!" Other than that he was a fine example of a student.

One week every year my friends and I go on a cruise. We look forward to it all year long: no housework, kids, husbands, jobs, or responsibilities. Some of us see each other only that one week the whole year. We have no desire to impress anyone or make sure we say just the right thing so as not to hurt anyone's feelings. No, this is a group of my very closest friends ("Peeps" as we call ourselves) who are from different towns and different churches.

Donny knows how important it is to me to go on this yearly boondoggle with the girls, and he always does whatever he can to make it happen. He takes good care of the home front so I never worry about leaving the boys with him.

One particular year when Zach was a senior, it was also hunting season. I knew Donny would be busy in the woods stalking Bambi during the day while Zach and Noah were at school. The first few days went well, but on the third day while Donny was in his tree stand with his gun ready to shoot a deer, his phone rang.

It was a call from the principal at Enterprise High School. "I have to give Zach three licks," the principal said (that's what a spanking is called in Alabama), "or I have to suspend Zach from school for three days." Yes, they still spank children in schools down here, even high school students. What's more, for you Yankees reading this, the principal and vice principal each have their own special paddles hanging in their offices as a silent reminder to every student who enters in!

The principal went on to explain, "Last night after soccer practice Zach apparently had to use the bathroom. Instead of finding a real bathroom, he decided 'to go' behind the field house." Boys, as you probably know, see nothing wrong in finding a spot outdoors!

Unfortunately for Zach, the high school had recently installed the latest surveillance cameras all over the school and property. When the security camera video was reviewed the next morning, there was my sweet son on camera, urinating against the field house wall.

Donny immediately told the principal, "Give Zach the licks."

The principal replied, "I really don't want to do that, but since Zach was caught in the act, I have to do something." And as men knowing what it was like to be a boy, Donny and the principal had a good laugh about it.

Since then, Zach has been very careful about where he goes! We've had many laughs about that incident and about Zach's security camera "debut." I'm not sure if it's made it yet to YouTube, but when/if it does, I'll be sure to share it on Facebook.

Don't be afraid to correct your young ones; a spanking won't kill them. (Proverbs 23:13 The Message)

WHO ARE YOU LISTENING TO?

I have been driven many times to my knees by the overwhelming conviction that I had nowhere else to go. My own wisdom and that of all about me seemed insufficient for the day.

Abraham Lincoln

Who are you listening to? Sometimes we listen more to what people say than to what God says. Even when we pray and get a word from God about what we should do, we usually ask other people what they think we should do. We seem to care more about others' opinions than about God's direction for our lives. Some of us even put our problems on Facebook and want answers from our so-called "friends" about personal or relationship issues. We should be asking God what we should do. One of my friends years ago told me, "Joyce, if you call all your friends about an issue that needs a decision, and they don't answer or can't talk at the time, maybe that's God way of saying you need to go to Him first, not the phone!"

Always asking someone else about guidance in our lives prevents us from being able to consistently hear God's voice.

If we're ever going to develop the ability to openly and readily have a relationship with God, then we have to stop listening to the world and begin trusting the wisdom God places in our hearts from reading the Bible and praying. True, there are times when it's important to seek wise counsel and sound advice, but always needing the approval of other people keeps us from discovering the perfect, divine will of God.

I see this mentality all the time in ministry with women. We so much want other people to agree with us and affirm what we already KNOW God wants us to do. I've met women who won't serve in the church until they discuss it with their friends. Instead of being led by the Holy Spirit, they're being led by their social clique. I had one woman recently tell me that I had disappointed her because she had put ME on a pedestal. Really? Me, on a pedestal? She was way off base because I'm so clumsy that any pedestal I'm put on, I would definitely fall off of, especially if I'm wearing my red heels!

Because relationships are important to us, we seem to have a need to impress each other with how "Christian" and "perfect" we are (at least at church). Problem with that is that no one is perfect. I'm not even close to being perfect, and I don't claim to be either! Yet, so many of us look around and think, "Oh, I wish I could be like her, pray like her, teach like her, know the Bible like her. I wish my kids were as smart as hers, wish my husband was as attentive as hers, wish my family life was as great as hers. She's wonderful, I'm not."

Come on, ladies! When I hear statements like those, I always say, "Don't ever compare yourself to someone else.

You are a one-of-a-kind beloved child of God, created in His image." When you scrutinize yourself in the light of others, you're unable to appreciate the special gifts God has given you. We all have special gifts, but if we listen to people and don't listen to God, we'll never develop our own unique way of serving our heavenly Father.

The devil wants us to believe we're not capable of hearing God's voice, but God's Word says that is not true. If we are believers, the Holy Spirit dwells inside each of us. God wants us to be led by His Spirit in a personal way and to hear His voice for ourselves. The Bible is the living, breathing word of God, meaning that it is relevant in everyday life.

Next time you want advice on what to do, ask God first, not your friends or Facebook. Start living boldly for Christ and don't be so concerned about what others think. Focus on what the Bible promises and where the Spirit leads. That way, when you (and I) get to Heaven, we won't have to explain to God why we did what our friends said to do, but we can be confident in ourselves and about the decisions we made because we trusted in Him.

Blessed are those who trust in the Lord and have made the Lord their hope and confidence. (Jeremiah 17:7 NLT)

The long prayer clock peek.

THE THIRTY-MINUTE PRAYER

When you pray in front of other people, if no one is there when you open your eyes, you probably prayed too long.

Donny Thrasher

Have you ever been in Bible study when it's wrapping up and you've already been there for an hour and half and someone says, "I'll say the closing prayer." How can you respond to that?

As a pastor's wife, I can't say NO even though I know the woman who volunteers is "the thirty-minute pray-er!" Her prayer is usually the same rehearsed and memorized prayer from "The Book of 1001 Ways to Pray to Impress Your Christian Friends". Now I know what you're thinking, "That's not right for Joyce to make fun of someone who's praying." Well, let me tell you! The pray-er is only trying to promote herself, not praise God.

She stands up and wants everyone in the group to stand and hold hands in a circle. Then she starts praying, and literally takes to heart the Apostle Paul's words in First Thessalonians

5:17 to "pray without ceasing." She begins with the weather of the day and then goes through the alphabet, praying from A to Z, from aardvarks to zealots and everything in-between!

By the time she's half way through her prayer, and we're only on the "L" names on her list, my legs have gone numb and I'm thinking, "When she takes a breath, I'll interrupt her, that's what I'll do."

For some reason, though, this lady doesn't seem to take a breath. She goes on and on and I've lost focus after the first five minutes. I look around the circle and see that not everyone has their heads bowed. Sure enough, others are looking around and they are rolling their eyes at me, pleading for help. The room is like a sinking ship and I am the captain. I have to do something, but what? I'm a pastor's wife and I have to cut off a prayer? That doesn't seem right! But I know it's just a show and the pray-er is using the words from "that book."

So I decide I'll butt in when she gets to the "P" names on the prayer list. Sure enough, when she gets to the "Ps" and starts praying for parrots and parsley, I realize I have to stop this. But how? So I say, "I have to go pee." Really, Joyce? That's all you could think of?

I end it real fast with that and "Amen." And I see all the women in the group looking at me in a very thankful way! I think they respected me more on that day than on any other day.

Remember this the next time someone asks you to pray: a short sincere prayer is just as effective as a long flowery prayer. In fact, when people pray those long flowery prayers, it reminds me of what Jesus said in Matthew 6:5-7 (NLT), *"When you pray, don't be like the hypocrites who love to pray publicly on the street corners and in the synagogues where everyone can see them. I assure you, that is all the reward they will ever get. But when you pray, go away by yourself, shut the door behind you, and pray to your Father secretly. Then your Father, who knows all secrets, will reward you . . . Don't babble on and on."*

The only person we need to impress is Jesus, and we can do that by being honest and real when we pray. We don't need to think of the perfect churchy words or what anyone else is thinking when we pray. We just need to talk to Jesus.

CRAZY SOCCER MOM

I am a shin-guard finding, uniform washing, Gatorade getting, picture taking, referee slandering, jumping up and down, always cheering Soccer Mom.

Joyce Thrasher

One season a year for ninety minutes once a week, I wear blue and white and wave cowbells. I scream, make hand motions (not always nice), but have never gestured to anyone that they were number 1 (that I can remember). I yell, stand up, and maybe call some high school boys and referees a few names. I don't act like a Crazy Pastor's Wife. I turn into a Crazy Soccer Mom!

I am "that Mom" nobody wants to sit by during the game. I talk too loud about the other kids on our team, how the coach shouldn't play them, how they aren't good enough, and on and on. I don't represent the whole pastor's wife persona well during soccer season. In fact, I'm sure some church members would be down right embarrassed to see me in action. I'm very competitive when it comes to sports and my boys.

I was the parent who always kept score at the YMCA soccer games when the other parents wanted everyone to get a trophy and come out a winner. Not me! When my boys were small, I was the parent yelling, "Get that ball! What's wrong with you?" I think it's good for boys to compete and want to win! Life is hard sometimes and we don't always get the trophy. Sometimes we don't get anything except a kick in the butt.

Donny isn't much better at soccer games! Don't let him fool you with his sweet demeanor on Sunday mornings. He can be as loud and as obnoxious as me at soccer games! He yells about calls the referees make and yells about our team not playing hard enough. He is so guilty in this story. He just won't admit it!

In fact, I guess there are a lot of "my" kind of soccer fans at our games because high school soccer referees across the state of Alabama voted our school's fans the worst fans in the entire state. That makes me feel a little better!

At one particular game, our boys were playing a team that was good, and our boys weren't playing up to their potential. It was driving me crazy! The referee is always a target for me, and even more so that night because I was so frustrated. I was taking every "bad" decision by the referee as a personal offense. Even though I didn't do it that night, at some games I've actually held up yellow and red poster boards to "help" the referees make the right penalty call. Of course, I never actually think they want my help, but it makes me feel better. I know they can hear me because I see them trying not to look my way. No doubt they wonder what that crazy lady in the stands is going to do next. I like to keep them on their toes.

At that particular game the referee did hear me yell about his calls on the field. Maybe I said some things like, "Hey, ref, you need an eye exam" or "where did you get your referee license" or "get your head out of the sand" or many other things I cannot print and will not tell. Yes, I was awful that night.

The game was in a large stadium and I couldn't see who the referee was. But I found out later he heard everything I said and could tell who I was by the sound of my loud, distinctive "Joyce voice." I also found out he attends our church! And to make matters even worse, after that game and my yelling, he decided not to referee any more games for our team because he didn't want to "cause problems in the church."

I apologized to the referee. He forgave me and continued to attend at The Grace Place. In fact, in spite of my obnoxious behavior he later professed his faith in Christ and was baptized. Did I learn any lesson about how we need to act, both in and out of church? Yes, I did learn one thing that day: before you yell at the referee, make sure he doesn't go to your church. In fact, every time Donny and I go to a soccer game now, I always look at him and ask, "Does that referee attend our church?"

At another high school game that season in a neighboring city, there wasn't a stadium. Parents sat on the sidelines so close to the field that anything we said could be heard by the players. Soccer players, even professionals and international teams at the World Cup, can be very dramatic, often falling down on purpose and then blaming a player from another team and hoping they'll get a yellow or red card. Sometimes players fall to "use up time" because their team is ahead. Soccer players who employ this tactic are called "Floppers." Let me tell you, soccer has a lot of floppers! I think flopping and talking smack among players is part of the game.

On that night I could see my perfect, peace-loving Noah run a little hard into another boy. The boy immediately fell. That took place right in front of me, so true to form, I started in, "Get up, Hollywood! You're a Flopper! You're just fine!"

It took a while for the boy to get up, so I had plenty of time to insult this 16-year-old. At that point I looked around and saw the other parents looking at me in shock and disgust. I pretended not to see them.

Our team won the game and later that night I received a text from a parent who informed me that the "Flopper" my son "barely bumped into" just had surgery for a broken arm . . .

Those who control their anger have great understanding; those with a hasty temper will make mistakes. (Proverbs 14:29 NLT)

"That better not be a second rib scar, Adam ."

AM I REPLACEABLE?

Work for a cause, not for applause. Live life to express,
not to impress. Don't strive to make your presence noticed, just
make your absence felt.

Author Unknown

The question I've been asking myself lately is, "Am I replaceable?" Maybe it's because I've often thought about throwing in the towel and moving away to a far and distant shore, changing my name, dying my hair, and not telling anyone where I am. But then I think, "No, I can't do that. The church needs me. My family needs me. I am irreplaceable."

Unfortunately, when any of us think we can't be replaced, that no one is capable of doing our jobs and doing them quite well or even doing them better than we can, we begin to see the effects of hidden pride. This is pretty serious business because God hates pride. We need to be careful and keep pride out of our hearts, minds, and mouths.

I encourage all moms (and all women for that matter) to take the time and consider this: do you think you're amazing and talented? Do you feel like a person who "has it all together?" Maybe you're beautiful, sweet, intelligent, funny, diligent, and so on and so forth. But don't think those characteristics are any of *your* doing. It's only by God's infinite grace that you are all of those things, or even some of those things. None of us should ever think we're better than anyone else. We need to realize, instead, that God gives each of us different gifts. He also gives each of us different children and none of them are perfect. Even if we tell everyone our kids are perfect, guess what? They aren't! Something eventually will happen that humbles us!

When my boys were toddlers, I was quick to say to a mother of older children, "I would NEVER let my sons do that." Guess what? I eventually let my sons do that! As prideful and judgmental as I was to that mother, I had no idea what she was going through until I walked in those high heels. And let me tell you. When you have teenagers, those high heels hurt and they are tight on your feet and all you want to do is take off those shoes and rest, but you can't because you have more praying to do now than when those teenagers were toddlers.

You see where pride can so easily step in through the doors of our hearts? We think, I'm a better mom than she is. I'm super mom, expert cookie-baker, awesome interior decorator, a wonderful organizer, the most gifted homeroom mother, the perfect wife, etc. Any and all of those comments can swirl around in our heads and before we know it, we feel we have arrived and have become irreplaceable.

I honestly wish I was irreplaceable. But acknowledging the cold hard facts of the truth that I'm not helps me face each day with growing momentum. It makes me want to strive to be a better wife, a better mother, and a better servant of the Lord. God has given me only a short span of life and I need to use every minute to honor Him.

This is the same for you. Whether you're raising a teenager who doesn't appreciate you right now, or wiping up a mess a 2-year-old has made, or being single and not getting married like all your friends, or having a husband who's difficult to get along with; whatever it is, you need to give it your best shot because you never know what tomorrow will bring.

I recently asked my boys, "If I suddenly died, would you miss me? Could you get along without me?"

"Mom," they replied, "really?"

They didn't like me asking those questions, but of course they would, and of course they could. What they didn't know is that I wasn't asking what would happen if I died, but if they would be okay if I escaped to an island with Donny and left no forwarding address. That would take care of everything and everyone, the church and the kids, but I wouldn't leave my cats behind; they would have to come.

As wives and mothers, we need to make our days on earth count. We do that by making time for what's important: loving and training our children to give their best to God, loving and helping our husbands in their everyday lives. We need to be joyful in every task set before us, not fake. Everyday isn't filled with rainbows and roses. Some days are awash with storms and thorns.

One day our time will be over – no more babies to rock, no more tubs to scrub, no more meals to cook. So right now, today, we need to whole-heartily serve God and cherish our families.

We are replaceable! So let's leave a legacy of love to our family and friends without a heart filled with hidden pride. We are useless to everyone if we're puffed up. We don't need to worry about what our friends are doing or compare ourselves to other women. We have enough on our plates when we look at our own lives and attitudes. The minute we think we're too mature or spiritual to make a mistake, we will. It doesn't matter how many Bible verses we know. The most important question is, "Are we living our faith everyday like we're true Believers in Jesus Christ?" Not acting, but really living, really making a difference?

I know there are some days when people see me at the grocery store, they would not believe I go to church, let alone be a pastor's wife! None of us have arrived and will not arrive until we get to heaven. So let's realize that we are replaceable, and for sure, if we serve with the wrong heart, we will be replaced.

Agree with each other, love each other, be deep-spirited friends. Don't push your way to the front; don't sweet-talk your way to the top. Put yourself aside, and help others get ahead. Don't be obsessed with getting your own advantage. Forget yourselves long enough to lend a helping hand. (Philippians 2:2-4 The Message)

"Scared me for a minute, I thought you were my Mom."

IT'S NO SURPRISE

In my experience, boys are predictable. As soon as they think of something, they do it. Girls are smarter. They plan ahead. They think about not getting caught.

Evan Colfer

Donny and I went on a cruise a few years ago and we left our "responsible" sons at home. Zach was 19 and Noah was 16, and Chris was in Atlanta only a few hours away if something happened. I had my phone with me, so in case the boys needed us, they could send a text.

One morning on the cruise while Donny and I were getting ready to go into Nassau, Bahamas, I received a text from the mother of one our boys' friends. "Do you know," she wrote, "that Noah threw a party last night at YOUR house?" Of course, I didn't know! I was enjoying the cruise and the Caribbean and trying to relax. I had no idea about the party and was surprised that my sweet, perfect Noah would do that. I was also surprised that my sweet, perfect Zach didn't stop the party. In fact, Zach's friends also showed up and joined in the craziness. Zach even took incriminating pictures of Noah and Noah's friends to show us how bad Noah was misbehaving!

When Donny and I arrived home after the cruise, according to the boys, everything was great while we were gone, nothing unusual to report. The boys didn't know that we knew. To be honest, the party really didn't surprise me very much because my boys are no different than any other teenage boys! I know you're shocked to hear that! After all, they are preacher's kids!

Donny sat the boys down in the "Chairs" and they cracked like eggs at a Waffle House. Zach showed us the pictures he had taken of Noah's unruly friends. In retaliation Noah told us how Zach and his friends had misbehaved as well. These two boys would never make good criminals!

Two years later Donny, Zach, and I were in Michigan for my nephew's wedding. Sweet, perfect Noah didn't go because he was visiting a college that weekend which he was considering to attend. Donny and I knew the punishment Noah endured the last time he threw a party, and since he was now two years older, we weren't worried. Well, guess what? We should have worried! Noah did it again!

This time he invited at least 25 kids to our house, all his "best friends." I later told Noah, "Nobody has 25 best friends, but when you advertise a party on Twitter and Facebook, everybody who is anybody will show up!" To be honest, I think 25 is low balling the number of kids who were actually at our house.

This time a video was made and passed around the high school by a girl using OUR HOUSE CODE to get into

OUR FRONT DOOR. The code was clearly visible on the video! She showed it to everyone because she was mad at Noah for inviting some other girls to the party. Always drama with teenagers! So now our house code was revealed on Instagram, Twitter, Facebook, Vine and whatever social media the kids use.

Next time Donny and I leave, we are changing the code on the front door and Noah isn't getting it! He can find someplace else to stay! Zach's in Auburn now, maybe I should send Noah up there. I'm sure the frat house will soon be having a party. At least it won't be at my house!

Noah is no longer left alone when Donny and I leave for a few days, and Noah does not have access to his car or phone. We drop him off at school and pick him up from school. Not sure how long this punishment will last, but I have a feeling it will last a long time. Donny and I have definitely learned our lesson!

But has Noah learned his lesson? Only Noah knows!

Discipline your children while there is hope. If you don't, you will ruin their lives. (Proverbs 19:18 NLT)

"Love the frat house Mom, even came with a cool bed."

THE FRAT HOUSE

Having children is like living in a frat house – nobody sleeps, everything's broken, and there's a lot of throwing up.

Ray Romano

When Zach enrolled at Auburn University, I think his only goal for the first semester was to be inducted into a fraternity. He accomplished that, but not much of anything else – not a good GPA, not even an okay GPA. So after the first semester, after Zach was placed on academic warning, he announced to me that he wanted to live in the frat house. Really? I could not imagine what his GPA would be like then, if he even had one. It easily could be 0.00, a new record at Auburn.

Since Zach had money he had saved from training with the Army, he decided he would "buy" his own room at the frat house. At his fraternity a brother "buys" a room from a former brother who moved out, graduated, or moved back home with parents. Zach picked out the room he wanted and sent a check to a woman in Connecticut who,

I assumed, was the mom who originally paid for her son's room.

Zach tried hard to sell me on his decision. "I won't have to pay electricity or rent," he said. "Food is free because two chefs cook three meals a day. We have a washer and dryer and even a 'House Mother' who lives here 24/7 and monitors the surveillance cameras. And I'll only be half a mile away from most of my classes, so I'll save gas money. And this is the best part," Zach continued, "my room is perfect because it's at the end of the hall and I'll only share one wall with someone else. It's really quiet during the week."

Now, does Zach think I'm that old? I know what goes on and what the brothers do at frat houses. I was young once. I went to college!

Zach wanted me to drive to Auburn with him (three hours away) and see where he would be living for the next two or three or four or five years (depending on his GPA). It didn't really matter what I thought because Zach owned the room now. As long as he was enrolled at Auburn, he could live there. Of course, that didn't make me very happy because what boy would ever want to graduate from college and work in the real world when he could just live in a room in a frat house. It was better than living at home with Donny and me. I certainty don't cook three meals a day. My guys are lucky to get one hot meal a day, and that is usually toast for breakfast!

But I made the trip to Auburn with Zach. I admit that when we arrived, I was impressed. The lawn of the frat house was manicured and looked well maintained. I was feeling pretty good about Zach's decision until we drove around back and parked. By the dumpster I saw a couch that had obviously been burned. Only the frame and coils were left. I asked Zach, "What happened? Was there a fire in the frat house?"

He replied, "No, Mom. When someone doesn't want an old couch, we just throw it in the pit and burn it." I didn't know what to say so I just shook my head and mumbled, "Hmmm."

We then walked into the frat house, and all I could see down the hallways were empty beer cans and red Solo cups. Okay, again, I'm not that old. I didn't say anything, but Zach saw the startled look on my face, so he assured me, "Mom, it's summer. This will all be cleaned up in the fall when everyone comes back to school. We'll have new pledges who will make it neat and tidy."

So Zach has two chefs for cooking and a bunch of pledges for cleaning. I thought, "Maybe I should buy a room here."

When Zach opened the door to his room, he just beamed! He was so proud to show it to me! I must have looked shocked because I didn't say anything for a few minutes. The room had cement walls which hadn't been painted since the beginning of time. The floors were composed of fake tiles and they were filthy. Zach's bed hung on huge chains from the ceiling. The shade was moldy. I went to the window hoping to at least find a good view. What I found was a broken window hanging by a single nail. The wall air conditioner had seen better days. I was astonished that my little boy, who lived in a lovely house with plush carpet, freshly painted walls, a cozy bedroom, and a clean bathroom, would want to share space with fifteen other frat brothers.

That trip to Auburn was beginning to look like the field trip I once took with Zach and his classmates to the county jail. The police officers showed the little kids the prison cells they would live in if they broke the law. I guess being scared straight didn't work because Zach was excited to be able to live in those conditions.

Zach then showed me the rest of the house. After walking through hallways smelling of stale beer mixed with sweaty locker room, he showed me a nice part of the house, the Great Room. The brothers are not allowed to have parties in that room. Finally, something normal! Then Zach took me to see the Trophy Room. I was a bit concerned when I saw all the panties hanging on the trophies, but Zach promised, "Mom, it's just a tradition. Not to worry." Really?

I felt I had seen enough, but then Zach took me down to the basement. There I saw a broken television set over the bar. Zach said, "Someone got mad about a game and threw a football at the TV. So now we have protective Plexiglas over the screen." Nice!

After the grand tour of the frat house, Zach and I headed home in the van. "Well, Mom, what do you think?" Zach asked. "Isn't it great?"

I sat there in the passenger's seat and just stared out the window, thinking about my poor son having to take showers for the next several years wearing flip flops every time. He would never be able to study with all the partying that obviously goes on in the house. Then Zach said, "Mom, why are you shaking?"

I didn't realize I was shaking, but I was. So I said, "No reason. You have a great place to live."

Zach moved this past fall into his room. He loves it! To be honest, I must admit that I was wrong. He's doing much better with his grades and he's "assured" me that the frat only throws parties on weekends. He's also in a weekly Bible study, so that's good. I guess he's okay.

At least he's not in a real prison cell.

Listen, my child, to what your father teaches you. Don't neglect your mother's teaching. What you learn from them will crown you with grace and clothe you with honor. (Proverbs 1:8 NLT)

SHARK WEEK

Our family put the fun in dysfunctional.

Meggie Thrasher

Chris and his wife Meggie are very adventurous, always look-ing for something exciting to do. Last year they decided to try scuba diving. They purchased all the latest scuba equip-ment, and even a pink vest for Meggie to wear. She looked like Scuba Barbie!

Chris and Meggie had a plan of action. First they would go to "scuba school" and practice diving in a "natural spring" of water, then they would go to the ocean for a "real" dive. They drove in from Atlanta to spend the night with Donny and me before this big adventure began.

It just so happened to be Shark Week on TV, and Donny and I had been watching footage of sharks attacking people. I even said some not-so-nice words after watching footage of the Megadon, the largest shark in the world who has attacked and killed so many people. He lives off the coast of South Africa, and unless he decided to swim thousands of miles to visit Panama City, I figured Meggie and Chris would be safe, at least from Megadon.

Meggie was so excited, telling me about diving and about her pink vest. That really worried me. What if a shark sees Meggie and thinks she's a big salmon? As Meggie talked, I listened, but being an over-protective Mom, I thought, "I need to tell her the truth."

Since we live close to Panama City, we're always hearing about sharks, which I have seen before with my own eyes from a hotel room on the beach. After going to the beach for over 21 years, I don't like to get in the water except with my feet, up to my ankles. To say I'm paranoid about the whole shark thing is an understatement!

I kept quiet about the sharks that night, but after having a bad dream about Meggie and her pink vest turning red, I could no longer keep my thoughts to myself. I think Chris knew what I was going to say because he gave me "the look." Even so, I said to Meggie, "Be careful! A lot of sharks are in the water at Panama City. Be sure and stay close to the scuba instructor. He carries a knife!"

Meggie looked at me wide-eyed and replied, "Really?"

Chris said, "Don't worry, Meggie. We'll be fine."

Then Donny gave me "the look." After two Thrasher men gave me the look, I knew I should be quiet.

As Chris and Meggie drove away that morning, Donny and I waved from the driveway. I then turned to Donny with tears in my eyes and whispered, "I really hope we see them again."

"Are you going to accept my friend request or not, Adam?"

FRIENDSHIPS ARE NOT
ALWAYS FOREVER

When someone says, "You've really changed," it simply means you've stopped living your life the way they want you to.

Carolyn Pote

As women, we often think that once we make a friend, that friendship has to last forever. But that's not always true. Sometimes God places a friend in our lives for a certain season, and often it's a hard and bitter season. That friend helps us go through the tough time and holds us when we need support, and says those encouraging words we long to hear.

I've also had several friends who came into my life for a season of spiritual growth and guidance. These were the women who prayed with me, held me accountable, and invited me to attend Bible study. They always had a verse to share to keep me on the straight and narrow. These were the women who expected miracles. But then, before I knew it, they moved away or just faded away. I think this was, and is, because God wants me to lean on Him and not on someone else for my spiritual walk. I do miss those friends, but I understand life is full of seasons and we all go through them.

As women, we often think we need to be responsible for our friends' feelings when something bad or sad happens in their lives. We try to fix those emotions even when they have nothing to do with us. But truth is, we can't fix anyone or anything. Sometimes we simply run out of glue and can't put Humpty Dumpty back together.

So why do we feel compelled to do what God does best? He's the only One who can fix anyone or anything. Yes, we can give godly counsel and pray with friends or pray for friends, but the outcome is up to them - and God. We can't get in God's way because we don't know if God wants to refine a person or teach a person to lean on Him.

Like me, I'm sure you also have had a few "toxic" friends, the ones who are always negative, make rude comments, have a better idea, don't like "sharing" you with others (I guess these women missed that lesson in kindergarten). These people wear you out when you're around them for any amount of time. They're not uplifting, and when you're with them, you feel bad or sad.

I've had two of these friends since I became an adult. I had to break-up with them and totally cut off the friendship because with toxic people, it's their way or no way. If they can't have ALL your attention, they pout, get angry, and basically act like a 5-year-old. The best thing I could do was make a clean break.

I'm sure there are some "Christians" out there thinking, "That's so wrong. We should be friends with everyone." NO!

We don't have to be friends with everyone. We are called to love everyone, but we can do that from afar, very afar!

Some people simply enjoy having daily drama in their lives. If there isn't drama, they'll make up some. As a pastor's wife, I don't need extra drama. Believe me, the ministry has enough! But when a friendship becomes a chore and not enjoyable, I still tend to feel guilty. Often when the phone rings, I won't answer because I know "she" is calling to talk about something in her life that's the worst thing ever. I've had some friends who were so negative that I brought that negative spirit into my home, and Donny and the boys were the ones who suffered.

The older I get, the more I know that friendships are not always forever.

I'm okay with that.

Many will say they are loyal friends, but who can find one who is really faithful? (Proverbs 20:6 NLT)

SURGERY FOR SUPERMAN

*Given a choice between the man of your dreams
and a plumber, choose the latter. Men who can fix your
toilet on Sundays are hard to come by.*

Erma Bombeck

I have always told Donny that he is my Superman. He always
believed me until that day when he realized some Kryptonite
was hidden in his cape.

In 2009 The Grace Place moved from its small building to its new, larger one. The buildings were next door to
each other, separated by a driveway. In the old building was
a Coke machine. Donny just knew he and two other men
could easily move that machine from the old building to the
new building. A fully stocked Coke machine can weigh up to
1,000 pounds!

Donny and his friends had a two-wheel trolley cart, and
they strapped the Coke machine to the cart. Then they
leaned the cart back a bit so they could roll the Coke machine
across the driveway.

Donny was on the backside holding the cart, and that's when my Superman knew he was in trouble. He didn't have the strength to hold the cart steady on its two wheels and had to set the cart back down on the floor. Donny also knew at that moment he had hurt his back. Not only did he know, but everyone in the room knew by the look on his face. He tried to stay longer to help move some other things to the new church building, but he was in too much pain. He didn't tell anyone he was in pain; he just told everyone he had to go home for a little while.

In the meantime my phone started ringing. First one to call was Dawn, a church member. "Donny really hurt himself trying to move the coke machine. He needs to go to the doctor right away!"

What was Donny thinking? Moving a coke machine? He's my Superman, but he doesn't have the strength to lift such a heavy object! I received a few more phone calls and by the time Donny drove the six minutes it takes to get from church to home, I knew everything.

Donny didn't plan on telling me he had hurt his back. He tried hard not to hobble out of his truck (but he did). Coming in the front door, he said, "I came home just to take a break."

I replied, "I know everything! We're going to the ER!" I took Donny to the hospital and sure enough, he had a compression fracture; but like the Superman he is, Donny preached two days later at our dedication service held in our new building, January 9, 2009. A week later he had surgery on his back and two days after that, he preached two times on Sunday.

This was the same Superman who was injured during Airborne School when he "miss-stepped" jumping out of a plane and hit his backside on the side of the plane (his backside is still numb to this day)! He didn't tell anyone about that incident either because he still needed to complete two more jumps in order to be airborne qualified, but he did them and he has a patch to prove it. Moral of this story?

God gives strength to the weary and increases the power of the weak. Even youths grow tired and weary, and young men stumble and fall, but those who hope in the LORD will renew their strength. They will soar on wings like eagles; they will run and not grow weary, they will walk and not be faint. (Isaiah 40:29-31 NIV)

BEHIND THE VEIL

The most beautiful makeup of a woman is passion,
but cosmetics are easier to buy.

Yves Saint Laurent

Don't think you're not doing what God called you to do just because what you're doing isn't as glamorous as you thought it would be. If you're a woman who honors God, no matter what He has called you to do, you are in the right ministry for this season of your life. Keep being obedient, keep looking for the next open door of opportunity, and above all else, keep a tight hold on Jesus.

I'm sure some people think being a pastor's wife is a glamorous job - sitting in the front row, raising perfect kids, doing whatever she wants whenever she wants (after all, she doesn't have a real job other than teaching a Bible study), coming to church only on Sundays, and sleeping with the pastor (well, some people may not think that's glamorous, but I do and that's all that matters).

Let me tell you the cold, hard truth. Being a pastor's wife is not glamorous! In fact, it's the hardest job I've ever had - long hours during the day, calls at home at all hours of the night, people in crises, sickness, hurt feelings, misunderstandings, plunging the toilets on Sunday mornings, taking the garbage out between services because someone put a dirty diaper in the garbage (and everyone is complaining about the smell).

One of my favorite non-glamorous issues is when Donny and I are absent from church on Sunday. Last year we actually missed two Sundays in a row for some much needed time off (or I was going to lose it and I am not talking about my keys or phone). When we got back to church, so many people said, "Haven't seen you in a long time. Did you have a good vacation? Hope you don't go away again any time soon. Must be nice to get out of town whenever you want." I just smiled and thought, "You have no idea, bless your heart."

Then I have my own non-glamorous issues, personally and emotionally, not to mention my three grown boys who need a mother on call at all hours of the day and night, and my husband who needs my attention (a LOT of attention). If anyone thinks I sit around reading my Bible all day every day, I don't.

Or maybe people think I have "quiet time" with God for hours a day. No, I don't, but I do have full conversations aloud with God all day every day, sometimes just asking, "Why? Why, Lord, can't you send me a cleaning lady? Why do I have to be a pastor's wife? Why do I have to be in charge of the Women's Ministry? Why can't Donny have a normal job?"

A Crazy Pastor's Wife

My days consist of the same things most women do. I cook, clean, do loads and loads and more loads of laundry, run errands, work at the church, buy food for the church pantry to help feed people in need, teach Bible studies, change the litter box, and attend soccer games.

I also go to the high school show choir competitions which are often five hours away from home on a Saturday night, yet I still have to make it to church for the early service on Sunday. Noah volunteered me to be the "Official Show Choir Photographer" for the yearbook when he was in the 9th grade, and I am now going on my fourth and last year of that job. Noah will be graduating this year and I will be retiring.

I also try to write a blog every week, but that rarely happens, and I also try to stay in touch with my friends. Sometimes I say to myself, "Today I'm going to have a normal life," but needless to say, that never happens. Some churches call their pastor's wife the "first lady." Not ours. I am the expert toilet plunger!

The next time you think about holding your pastor's wife to a higher standard, remember that she is human just like you. Probably just like you, she sometimes wants to run away and hide, but she doesn't. She doesn't give up. She isn't allowed to change her identity, dye her hair, or have plastic surgery so nobody will recognize her. She can't. She has a calling.

My calling to be a pastor's wife was not something I ever dreamed about. In fact, a few years ago my brother Joe ran into Rick, one of my "old" friends in Michigan. When Joe told Rick that I was living in Alabama and married to a pastor, Rick waited for the punch line! But Joe said, "Really. Believe me! Joyce is married to a pastor. Go figure."

Looking back on my life, I can see how God prepared me to serve Him this way. I love being a pastor's wife because I love God and I love "the pastor" so much!

God can use us in so many surprising ways if we'll only let Him. We just have to find our spot and learn to appreciate how God has gifted us. My spiritual gifts are encouraging others, acts of service, and leadership. While I enjoy using my spiritual gifts, there are times when I have to do something I'm not "gifted" to do, and those times can be difficult. But God expects us to step up to the challenge and serve Him at all times, even when it isn't convenient, easy, or glamorous.

Each one should use whatever gift he has received to serve others, faithfully administering God's grace in its various forms. (First Peter 4:10 NIV)

"Adam, I have a bone to pick with you!"

THE FORBIDDEN "S" WORD

*Freely use these six words that have the power to make
disagreements easier to overcome: "You know, you may be right."*

Author Unknown

Submission. Oh yes, I have said it now. The forbidden "S"
word!

But ladies, calm down. All submission means is to put
someone else first. The first one we need to submit to is
God in heaven. Then on earth we need to submit to our husbands. The Bible says if we submit to our husbands and his
decisions, then our husbands will have to answer to God for
the decisions they make. We're just called to submit to them,
and they're in charge of answering to God. How easy is that?

Not so easy for us women who have decisions to make on
a daily basis and on the spot. Our husbands may be too busy
and can't help, so we have to try to think like them! That's
not easy. Then when we make the decisions and our husbands come home and say, "Why did you do that?" That's

when we should realize we just need to submit at that point, or serve jail time!

Truth be known, our husbands have much harder jobs than we do. So many times I find myself not submitting to the small things in my marriage: what show to watch on TV, where to eat dinner, how to arrange the table and chairs in the dinning room. This has been an ongoing "talk" for several years in our home. Right now my husband is winning. When I have a hard time submitting to the small things, then it's even harder for me to submit to the big things in my marriage: paying bills, buying a house, or maybe even going to the church my husband loves (well, since Donny is a pastor, I have no choice in that). Not that I don't love The Grace Place. I do! And I go not only because I literally sleep with the pastor, but because I love the people there.

I know a lot of women who get mad about something at a church and they make their husbands leave a church, even when their husbands feel comfortable, and usually then their husbands are never faithful to any church again. As wives, we need to submit to God first and then to our husbands. If we don't, we may find out how hard it is to make all the decisions, both big and small, without a husband to help.

Submission doesn't mean we have no opinion or that we should be barefoot and pregnant and just stay home and cook and clean and take care of the kids, or that we should be a doormat. To the contrary, God made us to be a "helpmate." Yet, so many times we tend to be a weight on our husbands back and we fight them at every turn about what we think is right. Matthew Henry, an English Presbyterian minister (1662-1714), once wrote, *"The woman was made out of Adam's side. She was not made out of his head to rule over him, nor out of his feet to be trampled upon by him, but out of his side to be equal with him, under his arm to be protected, and near his heart to be loved."*

A wife should submit to her husband, not because she is inferior, but because that is how God designed the marital relationship. Submission is a wife submitting to her husband and her husband sacrificially loving her in turn. Submission is a natural response to leadership. But submission is not one-sided. Biblical submission is designed to be between two spirit-filled believers who are mutually committed to each other and to God. Submission is a two-way street, a position of honor and completeness.

As women, we must not disobey God or the law in the name of "submission." Some men take advantage of women using the word "submission" and the church. That is not what God intended and no woman should be abused or talked down to because she is a woman. A wife should be loved and honored and respected by her husband in the same way that Christ loves the church. Now ladies, that is some BIG love right there!!

Wives, submit to your husbands as to the Lord. For the husband is the head of the wife as Christ is the head of the church, his body, of which he is the Savior. (Ephesians 5:22-23 NIV)

"You did what?"

EYE SHOULDN'T HAVE LOOKED

Love is blind, but marriage is a real eye-opener.

Paula Deen

A few years ago Donny had bladder cancer. He had to go to the doctor every three months to be examined and re-examined. The only way bladder cancer can be visually checked is with the use of a camera, and there's only one way to do that! Yep, that's right! You can figure that part out. Not going to explain it. If you don't know, Google it!

One of Donny's appointments was at a cancer center about two hours from our house. The doctor was taking longer than usual to see us. While waiting in the examining room, Donny assumed the position so many of us women assume so many times - and it wasn't and isn't comfortable. It's a very vulnerable position!

I was trying to make light of the situation so Donny could think about something other than what was going to happen after the doctor came in. I noticed the Cystoscope lying on the counter. This instrument is a slender tube with a small video camera attached to the end of it. I decided to have a little fun with the Cystoscope since it was pretty boring just looking at Donny in the position. I pointed the camera at myself and could see myself on the TV screen in the room. Donny was telling me, "Stop it! What if the doctor walks in?"

I replied, "Well, he shouldn't leave this stuff lying around and then leave us in here for over an hour and expect us not to touch anything."

Wanting to have more fun, I put my eye close to the camera, real close to the very small camera with the really bright light. Donny and I were laughing because the entire TV screen was now filled with the image of my eyeball! Then Donny got serious again. "Put that down," he said, "or the doctor will catch you playing with the equipment!" I had to laugh because Donny was sprawled out on the table and really couldn't stop me.

The doctor soon came in, his examination went well, and we left. Because it is so uncomfortable for Donny after an examination, I always drive home while he squirms in pain in the passenger seat. As I was driving, my eye kept twitching and hurting. I had to shut it just to block out the sunlight. Thank God it was my left eye so Donny couldn't see it from his seat. But he was in so much pain, I doubt he would have noticed if I was driving topless (I wasn't and never have - I just want to give an example of how much pain Donny was in).

As soon as we got home, I told Donny that I needed to go to the ophthalmologist because I hurt my eye looking into the scope. My eye was red and watering and at that point Donny could see my problem. "I told you not to do that," he said. Of course, he was right.

When I got to the doctor's office, I had to tell him what I had done. The doctor asked, "Do you know where that scope is used and put?"

I replied, "Yes, I was there!"

The doctor left the room for a minute and then stuck his head back into the room. "Don't touch anything!" he said. Really? I guess that was fair.

So many times in life I think we all do this - look at the wrong things. Maybe we look at someone in a spiteful way and judge them, or maybe we look into someone else's business and talk about how they aren't doing the right thing. Maybe we should try to keep our eyes on our own lives and what we should be doing instead of on other people and how they should be living.

So the moral of this story is be careful what you do because you never know when you'll have to explain it later!

The eye is a lamp for your body. A pure eye lets sunshine into your soul. (Matthew 6:22 NLT)

THE LUCKY MAN

Never pick your husband up from work on a hot summer day naked in a raincoat. He may be running late and you end up waiting in his office with a raincoat in the middle of summer.

Elizabeth Pierce

One day I had to go to the doctor. Ladies, you know the one I'm talking about, The Doctor all women HAVE to see once a year. Donny went with me to that appointment and he came into the examining room with me.

The doctor was old, even older than Donny. While the doctor was doing the exam, he looked at Donny and said, "You're a lucky man."

My sweet husband shook his head in agreement and said, "Yes, I am."

The doctor then asked, "How did an old man like you get a woman like this?"

Donny looked at him and said, "I'm a lucky man."

At least two more times the doctor said to Donny, "You're a lucky man."

The exam ended, Donny and I went home, but over the next few weeks, out of the blue, I just had to use that phrase. I couldn't help myself! Ever so often, I would say to Donny, "You're a lucky man," and we would both laugh.

Fast forward to Valentine's Day, which was a few weeks off.

I went to the salon where I have my nails done and noticed that they were running a special for a Brazilian Wax! Now, I had heard of that, but had never had it done. Then my mind started going crazy, like it often does, and I thought, "What if I got Donny a 'Lucky Man' shirt and got the Brazilian Wax and surprised him when he came home on Valentine's Day?!"

So I made an appointment to be "waxed" at 2:00 in the afternoon on Valentine's Day. I had everything planned. Donny needed to perform a wedding that evening and he would be home around 8:00.

Two o'clock came and I arrived at the "waxing" room. I had taken a Motrin before and thought, "I can do this." The procedure began. It was bad, but I was dealing with the pain! Even so, half way through the wax, I sat up and grabbed my purse and started chewing, yes chewing, pain pills like M&Ms. Through my teeth I said, "Water! I need water!" By the time the waxer brought the water, I had already swallowed the pills. I couldn't stop now. I was only half way waxed. I needed to finish this. How lucky would a man be with only half the surprise? I made it through the rest of the procedure.

A few hours later, around 5:00, I wasn't feeling right. In fact, I was having quite a nasty reaction, blisters and a lot of swelling! I didn't know what to do, so I called my friend Lisa who had had one of those waxes and she told me what I was experiencing wasn't normal. It was getting worse and it was now 7:00. I only had an hour at that point to get ready for The Big Valentine's Surprise!

But I was in so much pain! I called Jennifer, another friend, and asked her to go to the pharmacy and get some pain reliving spray and ointment. I was in my robe, and there was no way I could put on my panties and clothes and drive at that point. Jennifer got the spray and the ointment and gave me some more meds, but at that point nothing was of much help.

Donny got home at 8:00 and to his surprise, he found me on the couch with an ice bag cooling my "wax." The Lucky Man didn't get lucky that night - or the rest of the week. But he sure got a good laugh out of my efforts!

A good woman is hard to find . . . Her husband trusts her without reserve and never has reason to regret it . . . She treats him generously all her life long . . . She's like a trading ship that sails to faraway places and brings back exotic surprises. (Proverbs 31:10-14 The Message)

A PROSTITUTE WITH SOME ATTITUDE

Everybody counts, or nobody counts.

Michael Connelly

God can use us in so many surprising ways if we just let Him. I once believed if God needed something "important" to be done, He would ask someone "important" to do it, someone who has it all together. God would ask the woman who never has a melt down at Publix, who is always dressed just right and whose hair is perfect and whose teeth are bleached, who always carries her Bible and knows where each and every verse is for any problem, the woman whose kids are at youth group as they should be and who are perfect teenagers, the woman whose van is so clean you can actually ride with her without throwing stuff in the back seat to make room. Isn't that who God would ask to do a VERY important job?

This may surprise you, but quite often God asks people who don't measure up to society's standards of "normal" or "acceptable." Instead, He asks people who will obey Him and will do the job He calls them to do, and be an example to the rest of us imperfect people He also calls!

In the biblical story of Rahab (Joshua chapter 2), God didn't call a "perfect" church woman. He called a prostitute who probably wouldn't even be accepted in many churches today. I'm sure she had a bad reputation and a dislike toward the many people in the city of Jericho who judged her. God could have chosen anyone, yet He chose Rahab, a prostitute with some attitude, to do an important job and protect His warriors!

Rahab lived in Jericho, a city which God wanted the Israelites to take over. The people living in Jericho weren't following God, but they had heard about God and how God had helped the Israelites win many battles. When the Jericho-ites learned that the Israelites were camped outside their city, they were concerned because they knew the God of Israel would protect His people.

Joshua, the leader of the Israelites at that time, sent two spies into the city. Rahab hid the spies at her house. Why did God use that "kind" of woman to do that? Because Rahab had faith (Hebrews 11:31)! She was willing to do what God called her to do, without hesitation. She was in a perfect position to help, and God could trust her no matter what she had done in the past.

Rahab was brave and tough and sassy when the spies arrived. While she was hiding the spies on the roof of her house, she told the Jericho army that the spies had gone the other way, away from her house. The spies then safely escaped and reported back to Joshua.

When God needed someone for this important job, He used Rahab. He didn't look into her profession or her past. No, God looked into her heart and saw her potential. Rahab probably wasn't very proper or educated, and I'm pretty sure she didn't dress just right or have bleached teeth. But God still used her, even with her faults and flaws. At the end of the story in Joshua, God destroyed the city of Jericho and everyone in it except Rahab and her family. They were spared because of what Rahab was willing to do for God (Joshua 6:25). God honored Rahab's faithfulness and included her name in the lineage of Jesus (Matthew 1:5). Can you believe it? A prostitute in the lineage of Jesus? That's right! Our God is full of grace and love for everyone!

Often I don't feel qualified to be a pastor's wife. I don't feel educated enough to teach a Bible study or to speak at an event. I think, "Who am I? What do I have to say that these women don't already know? I'm not even interesting." If everyone knew my past, they probably wouldn't ask me to speak or teach a Bible study. They might even shun me. But the truth is, God can and does use me for His ministry. He uses my past experiences, even with my faults and flaws, to witness to others. He uses my humorous way of thinking and looking at life to encourage and inspire others. Everything about me God can and does use.

I've grown so much over the years by letting God open the doors of my heart whenever and wherever He sees fit. I know God has a plan for my life, and part of this plan is to continue growing and learning more about Him and how to love and serve Him better. God can use any one of us if we're ready, willing, and able to be a vessel for Him!

Remember, if God could use Rahab for something so important, He can use you, too!

For we are God's masterpiece. He has created us anew in Christ Jesus, so that we can do the good things he planned for us long ago. (Ephesians 2:10 NLT)

"It's soooo hot in here."

HISSY FITS, PITY PARTIES, AND HORMONES

Always keep several get well cards on the mantel. That way, if unexpected guests arrive, they'll think you've been sick and unable to clean.

Stephanie Baran

Do you ever feel like you've "lost it" and just want to scream at everyone you come in contact with - at the doctor's office, your child's school, McDonald's drive-thru, the pharmacy, and the grocery store? Nobody is moving fast enough! Surely it's a conspiracy with everyone in the world trying to annoy you! I know I often feel that way. In fact, just this morning I felt that way and realized it was time to go home and re-group and come back out of hiding when I didn't feel like tearing someone's head off.

So now I'm at home with Noah and the three cats. Noah needs my help. He can't find underwear, homework, and the shirt he has to wear for a play tomorrow at 8:00 a.m. I forgot about the play. "Who performs at 8:00 in the morning?" I ask. Then I realize it's Noah's eccentric high school drama teacher and I think, "She does."

Noah's shirt is at the bottom of the laundry basket under the wet soccer socks from two days ago. The shirt needs to be washed and ironed, a real ironing, not just a go-over-with-a-wet-wash-cloth-and-into-the-dryer-for-20-minutes iron- ing. I'll have to find the iron and ironing board someplace in the garage that looks like an episode of Hoarders.

Donny arrives home about this time and asks the question all women hate, "What's for dinner?" I repeat, "WHAT'S FOR DINNER? Are you kidding me? I have to wash and iron a shirt that's now toxic due to wet soccer socks, and I have to help Noah find his homework for his Forensic Science experiment." His experiment, by the way, is taking place in his bedroom where he's trying to determine how long a half consumed glass of milk will stay good without growing fur. It's been growing fur now for over six months!

Then the home phone rings, and apparently no one in the Thrasher house knows how to answer it except me; everyone just looks at each other. So I say, "Don't worry, I'll get it." I pick up the phone to hear Zach calling from college. "Mom," he says excitedly, "I put my name in a bowl by the cash regis- ter at this Chinese restaurant and I just won a five-day cruise to the Bahamas. All I need is your credit card number to reserve it!" Really?

At this point I'm thinking about running out of the house and changing my identity, and then I remember something when I was a kid - my mom laying on the couch with a towel over her head mumbling incoherently, "Nobody cares about me, nobody helps me, nobody appreciates me." I would think, "Why is she crying? What's she talking about?" And then I remember that after I looked at her for a few minutes, trying to understand her mumblings, I went right on doing whatever I was doing and never gave her a second thought.

Now that I'm married and have a husband and three kids, I understand what pity parties are. I've been having them for years! Hissy fits, too!

As women, we tend to "lose it" not only in our homes, but in our spiritual lives as well. When I feel sorry for myself, the last thing I want to do is open the Bible and see what God says I should do. I know He would say, "Joyce, get up, stop whining, and go tell people about Me and how Jesus died on the cross for them so they can have eternal life in Heaven."

But instead of reading the Bible, I often go to my Facebook page, and I can always find something that makes me even madder than I already am. Any post that's on Facebook, I can take it personally, as if it's a post just to offend me! Then I'm not only mad at everyone in my house, neighborhood, and church, but now I'm mad at all my 1,546 "friends" on Facebook!

An older, wiser woman, Mrs. Elaine, who goes to our church and knows I suffer with the "Pity Party and Hissy Fit Syndrome" recently gave me a gift. It's a mug with these words printed on it: *I am wearing my Big Girl Panties, but they are starting to bunch!* That mug says it all because that's often how I feel. My panties definitely get bunched (maybe I should start wearing thongs).

Two years ago when I went to a doctor to see about hormone therapy, the doctor said, "You are peri-menopausal." That made sense with my mood swings and always being frustrated, mad, and hot at the world. She asked, "Are you growing hair where you normally don't?" Well, yes, on my chin, but I just pluck it (I thought it was a bit personal for the doc to ask that). The doctor wanted me to have some tests to see if my hormones were "off." Well, I didn't have time for tests. I had laundry, dishes, cleaning, cooking, and the boys and Donny to take care of. I never went back to that doctor. So I never got a prescription for hormones.

So I went through the past two years frustrated, mad, and hot - and hairy! I hosted a lot of pity parties and threw a lot of hissy fits! My mom, who has been there and done that, sympathized with me and said, "Honey, take this pill." It was a hormone. Desperate, I took the pill and I felt so much better! I then went to a new doctor last week and was prescribed my own hormones! Hallelujah! What a relief!

In fact, just the other day my youngest son said, "Mom, I like you better now that you're taking hormones." That was sweet . . .

Whatever is true, whatever is noble, whatever is right, whatever is pure, whatever is lovely, whatever is admirable - if anything is excellent or praiseworthy, think about such things . . . and the God of peace will be with you. (Philippians 4:8-9 NIV)

DON'T PULL THE PLUG YET!

It may seem strange to state,
but the very first requirement in a hospital
is that you should do the patient no harm.

Florence Nightingale

Disclaimer: Donny and my brother, Joe, advised me not to include this story in this book, but I didn't listen. After all, I am a Crazy Pastor's Wife!

When Donny visits people in the hospital, he often asks me to come along. If I'm not busy, I usually go. It's always interesting when we make these visits because we never know what will happen. I've seen a lot of things I wish I hadn't seen. When we make a visit, we ALWAYS knock and Donny says, "Hello." If we're visiting a woman, I have to walk in first so Donny doesn't see something that could scar him for life!

When Donny and I were first married, though, I wasn't accustomed to making hospital visits. I seldom went when I was growing up in Michigan because my family and friends were pretty healthy. But when I started going with Donny on visits, I always felt the "temptation" to pull the tubes out of people. Why, I don't know, maybe I needed to be in the hospital and on meds myself! It was just an "urge," and I really can't explain it, except to say that's why they call me a crazy pastor's wife!

Whenever we went to a hospital, Donny knew this "quirk" about me, and always got nervous if I got too close to a patient. The worst temptation usually happened when we prayed with a patient and we all held hands! Because there it was! The tube! Right there in the patient's hand! But I never pulled any tubes out or hurt anyone, so don't even ask me about that. If someone died after we visited, I had nothing to do with it!

Recently Donny and I made a hospital visit to see Jo Ellen, a lady about Donny's age. Jo Ellen had pneumonia and had a tube in her back. She asked Donny to look at the tube to make sure it was inserted correctly. Since Jo Ellen was wearing a flimsy hospital gown, Donny looked at me and said, "Joyce, see if that tube is in right." Like I knew! I wasn't a doctor!

As soon as Donny said that, I saw the look in his eyes that said, "Oh no, what if Joyce pulls the tube out?" Well, I looked at the tube and sure enough, Jo Ellen only had on the flimsy hospital gown, nothing more, with the back of the gown wide open! So I managed to save Donny the trauma of seeing what I had to see. But, thank you, God, I didn't pull out the tube. I just told Jo Ellen, "Yep, it's in there all right," as if I knew anything. Jo Ellen obviously was heavily medicated, and since she had asked her pastor to literally look at her naked backside, I thought that was the safest thing to say.

Now don't worry. I no longer have the "temptation" to pull out tubes. So if you see me coming into your hospital room, you don't need to be afraid!

And I promise not to pull the plug either!

No test or temptation that comes your way is beyond the course of what others have had to face. All you need to remember is that God will never let you down; he'll never let you be pushed past your limit; he'll always be there to help you come through it. (1st Corinthians 10:13 The Message)

THE INAPPROPRIATE HUG

Life is lumpy. A lump in the oatmeal, a lump in the throat, and a lump in the breast are not the same kind of lump. One needs to learn the difference.

Robert Fulghum

One day Donny asked me to go with him to visit Vickie, a friend and church member who was fighting breast cancer. Vickie was also only one of the few people, including Donny, at our church or for that matter in the whole state of Alabama who was a die hard Arkansas Razorback fan. We had been checking on Vickie regularly as she went through radiation and chemo.

Vickie had such a great attitude about her illness and was always positive. She never said, "Woe is me" or "Why Me?" Her attitude was, "Why not me?" It never fails to amaze me when people go through a situation like cancer and still find the blessing in everyday moments while others, including myself, tend to worry about petty problems. When someone is literally fighting for his or her life, it really puts all things in perspective.

Donny and I arrived at Vickie's house and she and her husband welcomed us in. After not seeing Vickie for a few weeks, I gave her a big hug and held her tight. She had lost most of her hair from the chemo and also a lot of weight. After I hugged her, I noticed she looked really pale. I thought, "Wow, that last treatment took a heavy toll on her!" Now I know why Donny had been so adamant about asking me to visit. Vickie was not doing well at all.

We sat down and started talking. "I've been in a lot of pain, and feel really weak from the surgery I had three days ago," Vickie said, "but I'll be getting breast reconstruction soon."

Oh no! I didn't know Vickie had surgery. Donny didn't tell me that. I thought she had a round of chemo a few days before. The more Vickie talked, the more I realized she had undergone a double mastectomy. Then I was the one who went pale!

I remembered the big hug I had just given her! Ouch! I was wearing a Victoria's Secret super duper power bra! You know…the one that gives some of us women a bit more uplift and a bit more oomph in the "endowment" department! Ouch again!

I then gave Donny "the Eye." Of course, as a man, he looked at me with a curious look like "what?" I didn't say anything more, just listened, and nodded my head a few times, thinking, "Why didn't Donny tell me?"

As we left, I was careful not to hug Vickie again, but I simply patted her arm and said, "I'm praying for you." When Donny and I got in the car, I looked sternly at him and shook my head, "Why didn't you tell me she had a double mastectomy?"

He replied, "Well, I thought you knew she had surgery."

I said, "No. I thought we were just visiting to encourage her after chemo. I gave her a big hug and she turned pale."

I felt bad all day about it. But I later learned that she was on pain meds and she didn't even remember us coming over. Whew!

So now when Donny and I go on a visit, I always ask him specific questions about what that person is going through. Men don't understand that women need all the details!

Ears to hear and eyes to see – both are gifts from the Lord. (Proverbs 20:12 NLT)

THE CATHETER

*Remember, as far as everyone knows we are
a nice, normal family.*

Sally Thornton

Two years ago during Thanksgiving week, Zach was still in Texas for Army combat medic training; he was not allowed to come home to Alabama. So Donny and I decided to rent a house in Texas and bring Thanksgiving to Zach!

We got the whole family together. Chris brought Meggie with him from Atlanta (at that time they were engaged). This was our first real family time with all three sons and our daughter-in-law to be. I was so excited to finally have a woman to help me cook! The men always sit around and watch football and don't even think about lifting a finger, unless they're sneaking meat off the turkey.

Since Zach was enlisted in medic training, he had "limited" access to equipment. When we visited him on post the day before Thanksgiving, he decided to smuggle some "things" in

MY purse. "Don't look at anything or take anything out of your purse until I get to the house tomorrow," Zach said.

Now remember, Donny is a retired Army officer and a stickler for rules, especially theft from an Army post! I don't know how I get myself into these predicaments! I was thankful we were able to drive off post without being frisked for stolen stuff.

I later learned that Zach had a plan!

On Thanksgiving Day Zach and a few of his Army friends came to the house we had rented. We ate dinner, which took a whole ten minutes. After Meggie and I washed the dishes, cleaned up the mess, and put away the leftovers, Zach decided it was time to implement his plan. He opened my purse and took out an IV bag with tubing and needles. Now I knew what I had smuggled! Zach told Noah, "I want to insert a catheter in you."

Given how Noah passes out when his blood is drawn at the doctor's office, Noah quickly replied, "No way, Zach! You're not putting a catheter in me." Even so, after much convincing from Chris and Donny, Noah relented.

Since I was the only mom and the only responsible person in the house, I made Noah lay flat on the floor (just in case he passed out). Okay, maybe I'm not all that responsible. I told Noah, "Let your brother put a catheter in you so he can show us what he's learned in medic training."

As soon as I said that, Meggie fled into the kitchen pantry and slammed the door. "I can't watch this!" she yelled. I figured she was queasy about blood just like Noah.

Zach began the procedure. I stopped Zach and said, "Wait! Not yet! Let me get the video camera."

Meggie yelled again from the pantry, "Are you kidding? Are you really going to video it?"

Laughing, I said, "Of course. That's what we do."

Zach inserted the needle and being the amateur he was in medical knowledge (remember, he was still in training), he forgot to smuggle an important item - tape to hold the needle in place. Chris came to the rescue and remembered seeing a first aid kit in the pantry. He yelled to Meggie, "Bring us the first aid kit!"

Meggie yelled back, "What happened? Is Noah okay?"

Chris laughed, "He'll be fine!"

After the procedure was over, I told Meggie, "You can come out now." I tried to show her the video, but she didn't want to see it. I thought, "If she can't handle seeing a little bit of blood, how will she ever be able to go through labor? I'll never have grandchildren."

A few days later we were all driving around in the van and talking about the catheter, and laughing. Noah had a small bruise where the needle had been inserted in his arm, and he showed it to Meggie. As soon as she saw the bruise, she let out a huge sigh of relief. "Oh my," Meggie said, "I thought it was a different kind of catheter, you know, the one used someplace else in the body."

Chris asked, "What kind of twisted family do you think we are? You've been thinking that's what happened for the last three days and you never said anything?"

Meggie replied, "Well, I didn't want to hurt anyone's feelings. When your mom was taking the video, I didn't know what to think." We all had a good laugh about her misunderstanding.

In our lives as believers, how many times have we done what Meggie did. We hear something about a person or a situation and we believe it to be true, even though it might not be the whole truth, or even any part of the truth. So remember this. The next time people tell you something or you think you hear something, check out the facts. Don't simply believe that people are right. Because truth is, they may be wrong.

Truth stands the test of time; lies are soon exposed. Any story sounds true until someone sets the record straight. (Proverbs 12:19 and 18:17 NLT)

OPERATION THONG

"There are just some things you can't unsee..."

Chad Boswell

Sitting in the front row at church, I see a lot!! More than I want to see at times!!

Donny always ends his sermons with a time for people to come forward and join the church or have prayer with a pastor or just come to the altar and kneel and pray. Many women come forward to pray at the altar every week, and since our church is very casual, some dress up and some dress down. Doesn't matter. Our motto is, "Come as you are."

Years ago one woman in particular always came forward to pray. She always wore "low" jeans and she always wore thong panties. How do I know that? Because I saw the thongs every time she came to the altar: pink, purple, black, red, polka dots . . .

There was no way I could let her show everyone her "stuff," so I devised a plan with Dawn and Sally, two ladies in our church. So what would happen if a woman was praying at the altar and needed "cover?" Operation Thong would be implemented! I would begin the process with a look at either Dawn or Sally, depending on which side they sat. Dawn sat on the right while Sally sat on the left; I had the middle ground covered.

When the woman was kneeling at the altar and showing God and everyone her backside, I would roll my eyes and tip my head ever so slightly toward that woman. Then either Dawn or Sally would execute the mission by going to the altar and hugging the woman and kneeling down and praying with her. In actuality, Dawn or Sally would be covering up the "thong." It worked very well every time.

One Sunday morning Donny and the associate pastor Chad were standing in front, waiting for people to come forward at the end of the service. Chad kept giving me "the Eye." As he moved his head ever so slightly to the left, I thought, "What's wrong with him?" He kept doing that and became more exaggerated with his eyes and head movement. I wondered to myself, "Is Chad okay? Maybe he has a tic or a crick in his neck."

Then I looked around and there was a young lady at the altar on his left who was not showing any thong, but instead, dear Lord, a plumber's crack, and not a small one! I mean, it was at least a few inches long! But it was too late to do anything at that point as Donny had just begun to end the service.

So let me give a bit of advice to all you ladies out there who wear thongs (or not). Be ever mindful and very careful when you kneel at the altar. People are sitting behind you, and you don't want to show them your thongs (or your plumber's crack)!

A Crazy Pastor's Wife

And I (the apostle Paul) want women to be modest in their appearance. They should wear decent and appropriate clothing and not draw attention to themselves. (1Timothy 2:9a NLT)

IT'S NOT ABOUT YOU!

The purpose of life is not to be happy. It is to be useful,
to be honorable, to be compassionate, to have it make
some difference that you have lived and lived well.

Ralph Waldo Emerson

Spiritual maturity is not so much about "what we know," but about "who we become." It's about learning to live and love like Jesus. Spiritual maturity is not how much knowledge of the Bible we have, but how we put that knowledge into use. Are our motives pure? Do we love people or do we feel superior because we know so many more Bible verses than other people know? But even if we've memorized all the verses of the Bible (and where to find them), the question remains: are we living out the verses and applying them in our daily walk?

After being a pastor's wife now for over twelve years, I've learned that many people in church who say they are mature, spiritual Christians often are not. In fact, the people who are truly mature and spiritual don't need to tell people they are because they live it and apply it every day. It's easy to see God shining through them when they serve others. They are the ones who smile even when they don't feel like it. They are the ones who serve in the background and nobody realizes they're helping.

Many times I've have heard people complain, "I didn't get anything out of church. I needed a deeper sermon, a deeper Bible study lesson. The music wasn't good today. I just didn't feel it." Really? If you come to church to sit in the chair or pew and expect everything to be about you, you're missing the blessings God has in store for you. The messages and sermons on Sunday mornings are meant to challenge each of us to serve others.

What about the new person who came to church and had never been to church before? Did you look for that new face to welcome or did you talk to the same people and sit in the same place as usual? I know "being unfriendly" is unheard of in the South, but it still happens, even here in little ol' Enterprise, Alabama.

Do you ever look around on Sunday and see someone who is hurting, a mother who needs help with her kids, maybe an older lady who would like for you to ask how she's doing because she's been alone all week at home and has no family close by? Or are you too worried if the Bible study is going to be challenging enough, or if the sermon is going to be deep enough, or if the music is going to be good enough?

Our goal at The Grace Place is to live and love like Jesus did. So instead of thinking about yourself on Sunday morning or talking about your spiritual maturity, volunteer in some way. Be a greeter at the door, teach children, invite a neighbor to a Bible study, pick up bulletins in the sanctuary after the services are over. Go to church to worship and serve instead of evaluating church for what you did or did not get out of it. It's not about YOU!

The disciples went hungry and thirsty and homeless while following Jesus. They were cursed, beaten, and persecuted for their faith and loyalty, yet they endured it all to bring glory to their Lord. They became the outcasts of the world because they loved Jesus.

If we truly love Jesus and want to follow Him like the disciples did, then we must serve others, not ourselves. But we mustn't expect earthly praise! We don't serve to be recognized by people; we serve to demonstrate God's love and to reach others for His Kingdom! Only then will any of us be able to hear Him say these wonderful words from Matthew 25:21, *"Well done, my good and faithful servant . . . Enter in and share the joy . . . Let's celebrate together!"*

My prayer is that what others see in me is a woman filled up with Jesus, and that His light shines through me and spills over into the lives of others.

Nothing in all creation is hidden from God's sight. Everything is uncovered and laid bare before the eyes of him to whom we must give account. (Hebrews 4:13 NIV)

COUGH SYRUP OVERDOSE

A pharmacist once said, "The best medicine for humans is love."
Someone asked, "What if it doesn't work?" The pharmacist smiled
and said, "Increase the dose."

Heather Boswell

One Sunday morning Donny was coughing a lot. It was annoying me so I imagine it was also annoying the congregation. I always try to give Donny medicine to help him feel better when he's sick, but like most men, he doesn't like to take medicine. He always refuses until I nag him enough, and then he takes it and it's amazing! He always feels better! But I can't brag about being right . . . because as women, we usually are right. I'm sure there've been studies to prove that. I just can't find them on Google.

That particular morning as Donny coughed his way through the first two services, I called my friend Sally and asked her to buy some cough syrup on her way to church. She picked up a bottle and brought it to me on the front row while we were still singing at the beginning of the third service. Because Donny was coughing so much, he agreed to take some of the cough syrup. He had already preached two sermons and still had another sermon to preach; I was worried he would lose his voice.

Without a spoon or measuring cup, he drank a little of the syrup from the bottle. "Not enough," I told him. "More, drink more."

Donny protested, but I insisted, so he drank more. I noticed the people around us watching their pastor as he guzzled from a small brown bottle in the front row. No telling what they thought!

But Donny continued to cough, so I persuaded him, "More, drink more."

He finally stopped coughing by the time he had to begin preaching. That Sunday at the third service Donny preached a better sermon than he had preached in the first two services. In fact, it may have been his best sermon ever! Several people joined the church that Sunday, Donny introduced them to the congregation, and then he said, "Amen."

After shaking everyone's hand, Donny came over to me. "My tongue is swollen and fuzzy," he said, "and I feel a little out of it, like an 'out of body' kind of thing."

Uh oh! Not good! I hadn't read the label on the cough syrup bottle. It contained alcohol, a lot of alcohol!

Of course, Donny couldn't drive home, and when I got him home and in the house and nestled into his Lazy Boy, he fell right to sleep. He had all the symptoms of cough medicine overdose (a.k.a. too much alcohol)! And come to find out, he had consumed the entire bottle of cough syrup because I kept encouraging him to drink more, drink more!

Geez, I was just trying to help, and he did stop coughing. His fuzzy, swollen tongue didn't affect his preaching at all.

Lesson for a pastor's wife: don't overdose your husband on cough syrup or anything else, especially on Sunday morning before he preaches (even though Donny did preach a better sermon the third time around).

The Lord God said, "It is not good for the man to be alone; I will make a helper suitable for him." (Genesis 2:18 NIV)

PASTORS' WIVES ANONYMOUS

A woman with any name other than "Pastor's Wife"
can rest on Sundays.

Joyce Thrasher

"Hello, my name is Joyce and I am a Pastor's Wife."

I feel like that is how I need to start every conversation with anyone I ever meet. It's as if I'm in a recovery meeting and must state my first name and what my affliction/addiction is.

Truth be known, I am, as they say, in "recovery." Not only am I a pastor's wife, I've also been a Sunday school teacher to little kids who wouldn't listen and who couldn't be disciplined. I've counseled women about things I had no business discussing, taught way too many Bible studies I wasn't qualified to teach (but nobody else would teach), have painted almost every room in the old church building, the current office space, and the food pantry. I've pulled weeds from the church planter out front and watered the flowers some old ladies decided to plant and then decided it was my job to "take care of" because they were dying (the flowers, not the old ladies). Why, I don't even have flowers in my own yard! I have rocks and lots of them!

I've also learned how to "play dumb," the best trick ever! My friend Sally from Mississippi taught me how to do this. I'm not sure I should share this in a book since some of you reading this will think, "Ah, that's what Joyce was doing with me last Sunday at church, playing dumb." I won't give away all my secrets, but it does help with the Mrs. I-Like-To-Gossip person. The scenario goes like this.

Mrs. I-Like-To-Gossip comes up to me on Sunday morning and draws me aside. She has a way of tilting her head down just a bit to get closer, and in a very low voice she asks, "How is Mrs. I-Just-Got-Divorced doing?" I look at her as if I'm a deer in the headlights and say, "I have no idea, I haven't talked to her, I don't know anything." That usually prompts Mrs. I-Like-To-Gossip to say, "Well, all I heard was. . .yada...yada...yada." And I say again, "I don't know anything." Then I look around for someone to save me and I say, "Oh, sorry, I need to talk with Mrs. I-Don't-Like-To-Gossip who is over there."

God only knows how many times I've used this "playing dumb trick," but it really works. I'm sure it's not politically correct to say "dumb," but it is what it is. That's what Sally calls it and that's what I'm saying!

Even though I've only been a pastor's wife for twelve years, I was raised in a church. Unfortunately, the church I grew up in was a very legalistic, independent Baptist church, King James Version only kind of church. Now if that's the kind of church you grew up in, or are in, I don't mean to offend you. For me, it wasn't the right church. All the women and girls in that church wore dresses and hats, and sometimes gloves! My mom made me sundresses for the summers and bloomers to match so I could run around and play without showing my panties.

Having to wear a dress didn't really bother me until my grandma, a rebel of sorts around the Baptist community, told me, "I'm not going to wear a dress to church every Sunday. I'm going to wear slacks. There's nothing wrong with women wearing slacks to church."

Then Grandma took me out and bought me my first pair of long pants. I remember them. They were cotton and a peachy color and I wore those as often as I could. I wore them out.

After Grandma pointed out to me about the joy of wearing long pants, I started looking around and wondered, "Why do these church women think they have to wear a dress, have long hair, look pious all day, and stay at home?" Grandma had always worked until she hurt her back at a paper mill. She was a tough woman with only an 8th grade education because she had to stay home and take care of her siblings. Her mother had epilepsy and fell into a fire and went blind. I spent most weekends with my grandma and granddad. They lived in the same town and always wanted to have us grandkids around.

I learned a lot from Grandma. One of the main things was, you only live once, so have fun! She got her hair and nails done every week by the same lady. Grandma dressed nice and wore pretty jewelry. She drove big Buicks, and yes, she drove a little too fast while listening to George Jones and Elvis.

Grandma often took my cousins and me on road trips. She was so independent and would just laugh and always want to be doing something. She didn't sit around much, now that I think about it. I guess I'm more like her than I realize.

When Grandma learned that I was marrying a pastor, she was a bit leery about it. I told her that Donny was 17 years older than me and a perfect southern gentleman. Grandma was happy to hear that he was older and from the south, especially since I needed someone to keep me out of trouble. When Grandma met Donny for the first time, she loved him! They just talked and talked!

But Grandma was skeptical about one thing. She thought we were Pentecostal! I tried to convince her differently, but she had her mind made up and when her mind was made up, no way could I change it! When Grandma learned that we had guitars and drums and bongos in our worship service, she asked, "Do you people also run around and dance and handle snakes and speak in tongues?"

I said, "No, Grandma, we have what is called a contemporary service."

She never understood that. She died thinking I was a holy roller. That is the one thing that always bothered her about my being a pastor's wife.

I am not Pentecostal or Baptist, Methodist, Catholic (but I did go to a Catholic school for two years), Episcopal, Presbyterian, Lutheran, or any of those man-made, mainstream denominations. I am a Believer in the Lord Jesus Christ, and guess what? That's good enough! I don't need a label and neither do you. I'm pretty sure some of you reading this book right now have decided to put it down because I've offended you. But that's okay. If I'm nothing else, I am true to myself.

Too many believers slap a label on themselves and on everyone else, not just a religious label, but a "Life Label." You know what I mean. Church people are the worst at this: divorced, separated, back slider, alcoholic, drug addict, cheater, liar, and the list goes on and on and on. But what those church people forget is that they themselves are gossips, self-centered, and not showing God's love because they judge others.

We need to move away from religious labels and personal labels and just have a label that says, "I AM A BELIEVER." But in essence, we really don't need that label if we're living life as we should. Everyone who meets us or sees us should see Christ in us! How blessed is that?!

"Can't hear you Preacher..."

THE OSTRICH SYNDROME

If doing the right thing was always easy, most people would do it.
Believers are called to do the right thing, even when
it's hard to do.

Donny Thrasher

Just because we have our heads in the sand doesn't change the outcome of any situation we're in! We can pretend that everything is great, but our country is falling apart around us. So come on, America! Let's pull our heads out of the sand! Because if we don't, I'm not sure how much longer our country will have any religious freedom, given the downward path it's traveling.

Unfortunately, too many pastors are afraid to preach about the tough moral issues in the Bible. Many churchgoers now hear nothing but "feel good" sermons - I'm okay, you're okay, everything's okay! Some pastors even use sermons bought over the internet. It amazes me that instead of turning to God for guidance and direction, these pastors turn to Google and other media outlets.

Joyce Thrasher

When talking to pastors' wives, I've been shocked to learn how many of their husbands won't and don't preach about the tough moral issues. They say their husbands are afraid of offending someone in the congregation! Really? Do you think Jesus never offended people? To the contrary, Jesus spoke the truth and didn't care what people thought. He was radical in His devotion for the Kingdom of God. He didn't just go around handing out warm fuzzies and pats on the back. No, Jesus spoke the truth and people were convicted and changed their ways. Yes, Jesus still loved people who sinned, but Jesus did not condone their behavior.

Truth is, we're all sinners. But we are saved by grace, meaning that we are forgiven, not because we deserve it, but because Jesus loves us and died on the cross to offer us grace. We all have issues and habits that we need to allow God to work on. We shouldn't judge other people, but we should stand up for what is right, for God and our country. As believers, we have taken a backseat on social issues; we have become too politically correct. We don't want to upset anyone by explaining what the Bible says.

It seems that every time I turn on television, believers are being targeted by Hollywood, schools, colleges, cities, states, governments, and the list goes on and on. Why are the pastors of our country not encouraging their congregations to be bold and witness to others, even if that means losing some friends or maybe even family members who may be offended by speaking the Truth? This happened in my family, and I'm okay with it. I'm weary of having to be "politically correct" and "keep the peace" so as not to offend anyone. Too many people get their morals fed to them by society's trappings and

not by the REAL Truth, the living, breathing Word of God, The Holy Bible.

I don't like to be an "end times" fanatic, but if we would spend more time reading the Bible as opposed to spending time on Facebook, Twitter, Instagram, and Pinterest (I am guilty of getting sucked into social media, too), we might discover we actually are, right now, in the "end times" (as the Bible prophesizes).

As believers, we need to teach our children that they are the future of America, and we need to empower them to share their faith and live boldly for Christ. Since Jesus died for us, we need to live for Him. We can't sit back and let God completely be removed from our country.

So come on, America! If you believe in Jesus, take a moral stand! Pull your heads out of the sand! Stand up and be counted - for freedom, for justice, but most importantly, for God!

Disclaimer: Let me just say that since I'm married to a pastor, I believe that gives me the right to write about pastors. Not that I'm an expert, but I do have some insight. I have not named any pastor or any church affiliation, so please don't accuse me of that. I am honored and proud to be married to a pastor who preaches the Word of God, not to offend people, but to reach people with the Good News, the Gospel of Jesus.

For the time will come when men will not put up with sound doctrine. Instead, to suit their own desires, they will gather around them a great number of teachers to say what their itching ears want to hear. They will turn their ears away from the truth and turn aside to myths. (2 Timothy 4:3-4 NIV)

"What's really amazing is that you can still see the dust in everybody else's eye so clearly."

REVEALED

Every one of us has the potential to change a person's life. We just need to take the time to listen, with our ears and our heart.

Carolyn Pote

The women of The Grace Place started a ministry to the ladies who work at the strip clubs in our local area. Our goal is to let them know that Jesus loves them and so does our church. We drop off gift bags once a month with lotion, chocolate, earrings, makeup, and a booklet to help the ladies understand God's mercy, grace, and forgiveness. Sometimes we include letters from women in our church who were strippers in the past or from women who just have a questionable past. We've also given each lady a new, pretty pink Bible.

I know my past is questionable, just like every woman sitting in every church in America on every Sunday morning. Even if we never worked at a strip club, we all did something we don't want anyone else to know about.

Our Grace Place ministry is to give hope to these ladies. We understand they are doing this type of work to survive, but God has a way out. God has a plan for each of those ladies. They can have new life if they choose to follow Him!

I so enjoy going every month to the strip clubs. Some of the ladies have shared with me the hardships they're going through. So many of their stories are sad about what led them to the strip clubs. Some ladies have children they have to feed and care for, along with paying rent and electricity without any help from the children's father. These ladies can't make enough money to survive by working a part time job at a fast food restaurant.

Alabama is one of the few states in America with a law stating that if a person is convicted of a felony drug offense, that person will be banned from receiving any federal benefits or cash assistance and food stamps. I'm not saying any of these ladies are "convicted felons" because truthfully, I don't know. If they are, the conviction makes it even harder on them if they're single moms. Alabama is considering lifting that ban and hopefully that will soon come to pass.

When we go to the clubs and talk to the ladies, I always tell the women from The Grace Place who go with me to not be a "Bible Thumper," meaning don't be someone who is forceful and aggressive in explaining Jesus and His plan of salvation. Now don't get me wrong! I do tell the ladies at the strip clubs about God and His infinite grace in a non-threatening way. Just like anyone else, the ladies won't care what we know until they know that we care. We must be consistent in our ministry, and every month help the ladies realize that we are here for them whenever they need us.

We've been going to the strip clubs for over a year now, and finally one night a few months ago we had a "break-through" with some of the ladies who had been cautious around us. That night the "girls" surrounded us and told us how much they appreciate The Grace Place and that they have never had a church reach out to them before. One of the girls told me she keeps the Bible we gave her in the front seat of her car.

Another lady who had been "watching us" for months to see if we were sincere asked us for a ride to church the next Sunday morning. Unfortunately, on that Sunday morning she was in pain from hurting her back the night before. She literally crawled over the floor to get dressed for church and even had to call a neighbor to help her do that.

That particular Sunday morning we had communion at church. This lady sat on the floor facing her chair with her cup and bread and prayed. I was definitely humbled! I thought to myself, "When was the last time I felt so bad that I had to crawl on the floor to get dressed? When I take communion, why don't I get down on my knees and pray?" This precious lady taught me a lesson that day - that I need to appreciate God and church more and not just on Sundays and that I need to truly worship Him, the Almighty God, who saved me from the pit I was once in and turned my life around.

Another lady told me, "I've never gotten anything from people without them expecting me to give something back." This makes my heart hurt because I'm sure that for some of the ladies, the gift bags are the first gifts they've received without being asked for a "favor" in return.

Most of these ladies have no relationship with their families. Many have run away from an abusive father and/or have been kicked out of their homes with no place to go. One night I met a new girl who was working. I say "girl" because she couldn't have been over 19, the legal age to start working in a strip club in Alabama. She told me, "My name is Star, but we use fake names for security purposes." After talking a few minutes with Star, she started crying and told me she was homeless with a 2-year-old son. I asked if she had someone to stay with and she said, "Whoever will take me home after work." I told her I could help her find a place, but she refused. "I'm embarrassed," she said. "I never thought I would be working at this club."

I told her, "Don't be embarrassed. We're here because we love you; we're not judging you at all." I invited Star to church and told her I could pick her up since she didn't have a car (most of the girls don't have cars). I gave her my cell phone number and told her to call me anytime.

Many "church people" only want to reach out to those with whom they feel comfortable, and usually that doesn't include strippers. Why is that? At The Grace Place we want to reach EVERYONE. We know that NO ONE is perfect because everyone is working on something (or should be). Our church, like all churches, is made up of imperfect people, including my pastor/husband and myself. It amazes me how people judge strippers, but won't judge the gossipers or the people in church who cause dissension.

If all of us would just love people as Jesus commanded, we wouldn't have time to sit around and be judgmental. In fact, Jesus said in Matthew 7:1-3 (NLT), "*Stop judging others, and you will not be judged, for others will treat you as you treat them. Why worry about the speck of sawdust in your friend's eye when you have a plank in your own?*"

No matter who a person is, or what his or her profession is, we should do what Jesus did. We don't have to approve of what people do to love them. Yet, sometimes with "church people," some sins seem to be more acceptable than others. Is that because we think we're better than others? We're all sinners saved by grace through faith, and it has nothing to do with how good we are, but everything to do with how perfect Jesus was, the Perfect Sacrifice on the cross for ALL our sins! To be honest, each of us is one bad decision away from losing everything we hold near and dear, or from having the same problems we judge in others.

Our stripper ministry is called "Revealing God's Love." The Grace Place has really accepted this ministry and we will continue to pray for these girls and reach out with our monthly gift bags and with anything else we can do to help. I encourage more churches across America to do the same in a non-threatening way. Just reach out and see what Jesus will do with such obedience.

We're working toward hosting a special day for the girls to explain God's love and also to follow up with them and help them secure jobs and move away from their current work. Please pray with us for the future miracles God is going to do with this special ministry.

I've learned a lot just dropping off the gift bags each month and speaking with the girls. I've also learned to get over the uncomfortable feeling of hugging the girls who are working in thongs. I just hug them no matter what they're wearing (or not wearing). LOL!

So now I (Jesus) am giving you a new commandment: Love each other. Just as I have loved you, you should love each other. Your love for one another will prove to the world that you are my disciples. (John 13:34-35 NLT)

"Face it Ralph, we don't text because we don't have opposable thumbs."

IDK TEENAGERS

Children are a great comfort in your old age, and they help you reach it faster, too.

Lionel Kauffman

Am I the only mom who texts a paragraph to one of her kids and asks four questions only to get back a text that says, "IDK, IKR, JK, LMK." He didn't answer any of my questions, so I text back and say, "Please answer my questions." In response I get back, "TMI, IDC, THX, K." Really? My four questions have been answered, but now I have to go back to my text to figure out what questions I asked.

Noah is the worst at this. When he needs money, he can write the sweetest, longest texts like "I love you, Mom. Do I have enough money on my debit card for a movie, dinner, and gas?" Hmmmm. Amazing how my sons' texts change when they want something. Sometimes they even call! In fact, when Noah needs something, he has the uncanny ability to find me wherever I am. Last year he went on a class trip to Italy and somehow found a way to text me and face-time me and ask for money! But when Noah is in the same town as I am and I text him, he usually texts back with IDK or no more than a one or two word response! Zach and Noah have also texted me from the bathroom needing toilet paper! What if I texted back, "LOL!"

This reminds me of our relationship with Jesus. It's funny that when we want or need something from God, we always know how to contact Him. We get down on our knees, place a "call," and talk for as long as we can about how desperate we are. Sometimes our calls to God sound like a 911 call (we never text 911; we always call). But when everything is going well, we don't text, call, Twitter, e-mail, Instagram, or face-time with God. I'm guilty of this and I know it's my sinful, selfish nature, thinking I can handle everything myself - until everything falls apart.

I'm convicted to talk to God every day and tell Him how much I appreciate Him and all the blessings He gives me and all the miracles He still performs. It's easy to get involved in my own little world and worry about myself and what I want or need, easy to get too busy to talk with God. But just as I'm still working with Noah about his communication with me, I'm still a work in progress with God. As much as I want my son to call me, God wants me to call Him even more.

Devote yourselves to prayer, being watchful and thankful. (Colossians 4:2 NIV)

STRONG WOMEN LAUGH

*Laughter rises out of tragedy when you need it the most,
and rewards you for your courage.*

Erma Bombeck

Some of the strongest women I know have the most positive attitudes about life. They are the ones who laugh when life is crumbling all around them (when most people would be locked up), yet they still smile and seem happy. They keep serving God and others. I know, though, they hurt on the inside.

These are the women who have overcome hardships and tremendous obstacles. Some have faced terminal illness, sudden death of loved ones, children fighting drug addictions, and/or a husband who walked away, leaving her and the kids with nothing because he wasn't "in love" anymore. Some have lost everything, and yet, you know what? They still smile and still seem happy and willing to console others.

These women are always there for you even when they're in pain. They find humor in not-so-funny situations. They're tough and gutsy; they get things done without making a fuss. They just move forward, quietly and efficiently doing the job God called them to do. They don't complain or say "woe is me" or lay around in bed all day. No, they get up and face their problems head on! These women take a stand for their faith. They aren't "politically correct," but they are "biblically right."

I've learned so much from the strong women who faced situations that seemed unbearable. One lady I talked with a few years ago had to sleep on the floor in an empty house with her 5-year-old son when she was eight months pregnant in order to get out of a dangerous situation with her husband. Now that lady is enrolled in a master's degree program and is an awesome mom, a shining example to her children. She volunteers in any way she can and is a role model for other women in our church.

I recently talked with a lady whose husband died in a simple, non-threatening, out-patient surgery, but she didn't blame God or play the "poor me" card. No, when she learned he had passed while sitting in a chair in the hospital room, she sang hymns. Yes, she sang to Jesus!

I could go on and on about the strong women I've had the privilege of working with and worshiping with and learning from over the years. They don't like to talk about their problems and they don't need any attention. They're confident that God has a bigger and better plan than any plan of theirs could ever be.

These women have taught me to hold my head high and accept the fact that life isn't always fair and never perfect.

When life does give me a good swift kick, I try not to let it get me down because there's always tomorrow. God has a plan for each and every one of us for each and every day. If we focus on a problem and stay tied to our past, how can we move forward into the promise of our future? We can't! So we need to strap on our spiritual armor and do what we have to do, even if we don't want to do it!

We need to face our battles like the women of God we are, strong and courageous! After all, the battles are HIS anyway and He will fight them for us, but we have to be obedient and not give up. As Philippians 3:15-16 (The Message) says, *"Let's keep focused on that goal, those of us who want everything God has for us. If any of you have something else in mind, something less than total commitment, God will clear your blurred vision – you'll see it yet! Now that we're on the right track, let's stay on it."*

THE FIVE -SECOND RULE

Things are not always as they appear to be.

Donny Thrasher

I'm going to brag about my brother Joe who illustrated this book with his cartoons. Joe put up with my nagging emails, calls, and texts ever since we decided to collaborate. I would write a story and send it to Joe, and since he's an "artist," he would decide if he "wanted" to illustrate the story with a cartoon. Artists can be very temperamental. But I love Joe just the way he is with his eccentric ways and all. Some of the stories I had to talk him into illustrating.

It's been so much fun working with Joe. The only obstacle we have is the 898 miles between us. He lives in Michigan and I live in LA (Lower Alabama). I appreciate all the time he put into helping make my dream of writing a book a reality. But he's still my brother and since I'm the author, I thought I would have some fun and tell you a little story about him.

Joe loves sweets! When he's able to visit, he's always eating the candy bars, gummy bears, and any other sugary goodies I have around the house. He's the one who ate the gooey gummy bears the cat "watered."

When Joe was dating his wife, Robin, one day he was at her house visiting. She had a small gumball machine setting on a table in the living room. Joe, being the candy lover he is, cranked the machine, got a handful of gumballs, and threw them into his mouth. He started chewing the gumballs and realized something was wrong. "What's up with these gumballs?" Joe asked. "They taste really gritty and have a weird, fuzzy texture."

At that point Sara, Robin's little daughter, spoke up. "Oh no, they're okay," she said. "I poured the gumballs out on the bathroom floor 'cause I wanted to count them. Then I picked them all up and put them back in the machine."

Needless to say, Joe immediately spit the gumballs out and washed his mouth out! With the gummy bear incident and now the gumball incident, Joe may want to be careful about what kind of candy or gum he puts in his mouth!

Eat honey, my son, for it is good; honey from the comb is sweet to your taste. (Proverbs 24:13 NIV)

IN CLOSING

I wish I could say I have this "mom" thing perfected, but I
don't. I don't have all the answers (when something happens
to my boys) and many times I don't have any answers. But
there's one thing I know for sure: I must do what God asks
me to do as a mom, and that is to pray, pray, pray for my Chris
and Zach and Noah. I believe this is a "commandment" for
moms everywhere to pray for their children, whether they're
leaving home to start kindergarten, leaving home to start college, or leaving home to marry and start a new family.

I also wish I could say I have this "pastor's wife" thing
perfected, but I don't. It hasn't always been easy, and it isn't
always easy! My husband gives me a reason to smile, laugh,
and hug, to be proud of, silly with, and available for, but he
sometimes drives me crazy and we have disagreements. But

there's one thing I know for sure: I must do what God asks me to do as a wife, and that is to pray, pray, pray for my Donny.

Oh, and one more thing I know for sure: God, our heavenly Father, loves Donny and Chris and Zach and Noah so much more than I do. He has designed a plan for each of us, a plan far better than anything we can ever imagine. My job is to allow God's perfect, divine will to be revealed in my family's life, both for now and for always.

I no longer count on my own goodness or my ability to obey God's law, but I trust Christ to save me. For God's way of making us right with himself depends on faith. As a result, I can really know Christ and experience the mighty power that raised him from the dead. I can learn what it means to suffer with him, sharing in his death, so that, somehow, I can experience the resurrection from the dead!

I don't mean to say I have already achieved these things or that I have already reached perfection! But I keep working toward that day when I will finally be all that Christ Jesus saved me for and wants me to be. No, dear friends, I am still not all I should be, but I am focusing all my energies on this one thing: Forgetting the past and looking forward to what lies ahead, I strain to reach the end of the race and receive the prize for which God, through Christ Jesus, is calling us up to heaven. (Philippians 3:9-14 NLT)

JOYCE THRASHER, a wife, mother, friend, writer, and motivational speaker, was born and raised in Kalamazoo, Michigan. She has lived in Enterprise, Alabama, for the past 21 years. Joyce's husband, Donny, retired from the U.S. Army after 29 years of service as an intelligence officer and a chaplain.

Joyce and Donny have been serving since 2005 at The Grace Place Church (www.mygpchurch.com), a fast-growing 2,000+ member church. Joyce is also the Director of Women's Ministries, teaches Bible studies, volunteers at the church's food pantry/clothes closet, and helps with many other programs and projects at the church. In addition to her hands-on service, Joyce reaches out to women via her humorous and inspirational blog on the website, www.crazypastorswife.com. Donny and Joyce have three sons and three cats.

We put the FUN in Dysfunctional

THE ILLUSTRATOR

JOE BROWN (Joyce's brother) has been a lifelong artist initially pursuing freelance cartooning and then "real art" with pastels (www.joebrownart.com). The real art phase grew into representation at numerous galleries and shows and numerous awards. Joe recently returned to cartooning, represented by Cartoonstock in London, England. He hopes to help people smile and maybe lighten their loads through humor.

This is Joe's 6th book of illustrations, but he first had to cooperate with Joyce who convinced him to help or she would tell Mom it was him who pushed her off the bunk bed and sent her to the hospital when she was 5.

Joe Brown and Joyce Thrasher

Angela Crowe Photography